D0952672

BY WES MOORE

The Other Wes Moore

The Work

The Work

The Work

The Search for a Life That Matters

Wes Moore

SPIEGEL & GRAU

NEW YORK

Published in the United States by Spiegel & Grau, an imprint of The Random House Publishing Group, a division of Random House LLC, a Penguin Random House Company, New York.

SPIEGEL & GRAU and the HOUSE colophon are registered trademarks of Random House LLC.

Library of Congress Cataloging-in-Publication Data
Moore, Wes.
The work : my search for a life that matters / Wes Moore.
pages cm
ISBN 978-0-8129-9357-8 (hardback)—ISBN 978-0-679-64601-3
1. Moore, Wes, 1978– 2. Moore, Wes, 1978—Career in the military. 3. Moore, Wes, 1978—Career in finance. 4. Moore, Wes, 1978—Career in television broadcasting. 5. African American men—Biography. 6. Baltimore (Md.)—Biography. I. Title.
F189.B153M67 2014
975.2'6043092—dc 3
[B]
2013038679

Printed in the United States of America on acid-free paper

www.spiegelandgrau.com

2 4 6 8 9 7 5 3 1

First Edition

Book design by Caroline Cunningham

To my wife, Dawn. You are my light.
Thank you for helping me find my "work"
and giving me the strength to go after it.

Everybody can be great. Because everybody can serve.

—DR. MARTIN LUTHER KING, JR.

Contents

■ ■ ■ ■ ■ ■ ■ ■ ■ ■ ■ ■ ■ ■ ■ ■

Introduction

Work to Do

As a soldier, you never forget the first time you get shot at. A sudden, stunning commotion engulfs you—the sound of shells buzzing past your ears, a flurry of divots leaping out of the earth around your feet—but then everything slows down as your training kicks in:

Find cover.
Scan for the position of your men.
Return fire.

Those moves don't come quite as instinctually as they did during training, but only because it takes a few surreal moments to sink in that this is real. That today you might die.

Moments before those first shots came at me, I was convinced that I was prepared for the experience. The idea of being shot was not novel to me; in fact, I'd been anticipating it for years. I had felt the possibility of death, tickling my neck like the blade of a guil-lotine, as long as I could remember. As a kid in Baltimore and the Bronx during the homicidal height of the so-called crack era, I would lie in bed on some nights and listen to the pop of low-caliber guns somewhere beyond my window. I'd think about who was squeezing the trigger, who was trying to get away from the speeding bullet; I feared that one day I'd be the one running from the gun—or holding it.

More recently, I had been thinking about shots and shooters as I trained for war. My paratroopers worked over and over again on perfecting "reaction to contact" missions. These were missions whose point was to maneuver in sight of the enemy until they de-cided to "engage"—a nice euphemism for "shoot at us with assault weapons"—which would reveal their positions and other intel. These were high-stakes missions, which is why we ran the drill so often. Even in training our weapons were loaded. In airborne training, we leaped out of planes in full "battle rattle," complete with a rucksack packed with gear and an M-4 rifle, as if engage-ment with the enemy could begin as soon as the balls of our feet hit the ground—or sooner.

There's an idea out there that a successful soldier is fearless. That's not quite right. Soldiers cultivate a certain amount of fatal-ism in our training; we try as best we can to assimilate the idea of our own mortality into our daily lives. We're all going to die one day—everyone knows that. As soldiers, we practice owning that truth, living with it, and, when the bullets fly, confronting it with calm professionalism. We knew there was a very good chance we'd be shot at when we got to Afghanistan. Even so, when I heard those first bullets, for a moment I felt my body flood with fear and tried not to let the fear control me.

When the situation was under our control—after we'd responded with overwhelming force, as we'd been trained to—the disciplined calm I'd forced onto myself vanished and a wild adrenaline rushed into me, the kind that streamlines and clarifies your perception and turns everything crystalline, if only for a moment. I walked away from that firefight alive and desperately thankful. But when you find yourself clutching on to your life like it's the only thing that matters—because you suddenly realize it is—you start to ask other questions, too. For instance: *why* does my life matter? While deployed, I had to let those deeper, existential questions pass right through me, because my only duty in uniform was to my mission and to my fellow soldiers. But in that moment of proximity to my own mortality, it was clear to me that I'd eventually have a bigger question to confront.

There were other times in my life—before and after that moment—when this same question arose, if not always with the same explosive force. It's a question that for some of us arises every day, often in a nagging, unfocused way that might leave us depressed or paralyzed because we don't know how to answer it; sometimes we don't even know where to begin. It's a question that might hit you in a foxhole, on the day after graduation, or on your daily commute to work. It hit me in every one of those moments and wouldn't let me go—and eventually I started to piece together the lessons of my own life and the lives of the people who inspired me the most, and I started to answer it.

I've been unusually fixated on questions of fate and meaning from the time I was young. I began to formally explore questions of success and failure when I wrote my first book. It was called *The Other Wes Moore* and it told the story of my childhood and that of another young man who shared my name. We lived in the same city, sometimes only blocks apart, and we were close in age. Our lives shared deeper similarities as well: lack of resources, fatherlessness, general delinquency, and unrealized potential. *The Other Wes Moore* was, at its core, a narrative exploration of what makes the difference between success and failure for young people in our society. At the end of the book, the two boys stood at the precipice of adulthood: I was leaving for Oxford University in England on a Rhodes Scholarship, where I would begin the next phase of my life; the other Wes was confined to a six-by-eight-foot box in a maximum-security prison, the cell he will almost certainly die in. The question I tried to figure out in that book was why.

This new book picks up my story where *The Other Wes Moore* left off—from the day I landed in England to the day, ten years later, when I returned home to Baltimore, and all that happened between that departure and homecoming: my time in combat in Afghanistan, in the bureaucratic war zone of the White House, in the Gulf after Hurricane Katrina, in China and India, witnessing and participating in Barack Obama's historic campaign, on Wall Street during the agonies of a historic crisis, and now working as a social entrepreneur leading a new grassroots start-up, with all the excitement and risk that entails.

I'll also tell stories of people I've met along the way, changemakers who've taught me some incredibly valuable lessons about what it means to create lives that matter. And just like my last book, this book uses these stories—against the backdrop of some of the crucial moments of the last decade—as a way of exploring the meaning of success in a volatile, difficult, and seemingly anchorless world. The great theologian Howard Thurman famously said, "Don't ask what the world needs. Ask what makes you come alive and go do it. Because what the world needs is people who come alive." If *The Other Wes Moore* was a book about how to survive childhood, *The Work* is a book about what comes next: it's about how we come alive.

That first bullet arrived months after my division completed its training in the blisteringly hot Georgia summer of 2005. On our last day of training we performed our final drills: how to relay a position to target for rescue or air cover; how to search for land mines and IEDs; how to say goodbye to family and friends. The next morning we flew from Fort Benning, Georgia, on a commercial flight bound for Germany, where we would stay for a night; in the morning we boarded a C-171 transport plane and hours later were making our final approach to one of the most dangerous places in the world.

When we off-loaded the plane, I was physically exhausted from the day of travel but excited to finally be on the ground. Bagram Airfield was an oasis for American soldiers—it was even bigger and more secure than I'd thought it would be. But the other soldiers knew better than me that the relative peace of Bagram would be an exception on our tour.

As if to drive that point home, after disembarking we entered the massive doors of the Tillman USO Center in Bagram, named after Pat Tillman. Tillman was the former Arizona Cardinals player who gave up his football career after 9/11 to join the Army Rangers and fight in Afghanistan. Corporal Tillman had been killed in combat a year earlier, shot to death by other American soldiers in the fog of an intense firefight close to the Pakistan border. I looked around at my unit as we in-processed into the Tillman Center. They were a mixed bunch, NCOs and officers, some from the depths of the inner city and some from places so small and isolated that they could name everyone in their town. None of us had left a lucrative NFL career to join the Armed Forces, but I knew that many of them—of us—were inspired by the same passion that had driven Tillman: to answer in some concrete way an impulse awakened in us by the events of 9/11.

We remember 9/11 as a day of chaos and horror, but the events around 9/11 also rewrote the script for the American hero. In the days after the attacks, the news coverage and newspapers were filled with images of firefighters and police officers running to their own deaths without a second thought, driven to action by an abstract idea, an ideal, really, of what a community is about: that our lives are all tied together in a bond of mutual dependence and mutual aid, and that in moments of peril we can save each other, or at least try to.

That spirit of service radiated from the ruins of the World Trade Center in the days that followed, but as time passed and our routines resumed, many of us struggled to figure out what to do with all of those feelings. My unit was full of young men and women who came of age with the image of the towers falling, of the hole in the ground left in Shanksville, Pennsylvania, and of military personnel carrying bodies out of the Pentagon. When I asked them about their motivation for joining the military and, now, preparing to deploy to a country almost seven thousand miles away from home as part of a broader mission that many of us didn't fully understand, the answer was often simple: they felt like it was their time to do their part.

■ ■ ■

The idea that we want to do our part—but are unsure of exactly how to do it—is not unusual. We start off our adult lives full of ideas about how we want to live, how we want to contribute to the greater good—how we want to do our part—but are immediately presented with the thorny puzzle of figuring out how to marry our instincts to action.

When we are children our lives are relentlessly paced—someone tells us when to get up, when to go to bed, when to eat, when to study. I have two beautiful children under the age of four and their calendars are already stuffed with activities. But something important shifts in the way we live almost from the moment we leave school. Our adult lives begin with a first moment of stillness. We leave school and there's no next grade to go to, no one to tell us how to spend our time—we are faced with an intimidating absence of inevitable next steps. Possibilities and choices suddenly abound. And for a lot of us it's terrifying.

There was once a clear answer to this terror. It used to be that we could extend childhood's safe rhythms by burrowing deep into large institutions—the military or a corporation or a university or the government—and moving up the ranks, like a kid getting passed from grade to grade. This brought a measure of security, but it required submerging yourself in an institution and letting that institution's logic guide the most productive moments of your life. This was in many ways the contract I was brought up to believe in.

But my generation was among the last raised to believe there was a way to cheat the blank future by burrowing ourselves in paternal institutions and following the traditional paths. We are now confronted by a world where those institutions are in crisis—and where the old model of work has been thrown open, not only because so many forces (robotics, the Web, big data, a global labor market) are conspiring to eliminate jobs and even whole industries, but because many of the jobs that remain can feel unsatisfying on a personal level. David Graeber, an anthropologist and activist, recently wrote this about the contemporary state of work: "Huge swathes of people, in Europe and North America in particular, spend their entire working lives performing tasks they secretly believe do not really need to be performed. The moral and spiritual damage that comes from this situation is profound. It is a scar across our collective soul. . . . How can one even begin to speak of dignity in labour when one secretly feels one's job should not exist?"

This has created a great deal of angst for all of us who've had to live through these shifts. But it's also created a greater sense of urgency around the task of designing our own lives to tap into our own specific ideals, talents, and resources—to find ways of not just working to live, but *finding the work of our lives*.

The people whose stories I tell in this book have done just that, whether it was Michael Hancock, who found his impact in the place he spent much of his life running away from, or Joe Manko learning that change happens one hug at a time. They've also discovered that the great work we have in this life is really to take care of each other—whether it was John Galina and Dale Beatty showing that service is a path to healing the scars of war, or Cara, Darr, and Tom Aley showing that capitalism doesn't have to be a zero-sum blood sport but can be channeled as a creative force for good.

For all of them—and for me—finding the work of their lives came back to that idea of doing our part. Success and service are increasingly intertwined. To be clear, service doesn't necessarily

mean running for office, suiting up in a military uniform, or vol-
unteering at a charity—although it might. Service simply means
we embrace the possibility of living for more than ourselves. After
talking with thousands of people across this country over the last
few years—hearing their stories and joining many of them in their
service projects—I'm convinced that most of the time, *that's* what
the voice inside of us is telling us to do. *To live for more than ourselves.* It's the truth that hunts us down, our common calling. And
when we answer that call, we'll find that the world's challenges and
our own work inevitably meet.

This book is not a how-to guide. Finding my work was not a matter of following prescribed steps—it was, and is, an ongoing journey, not a ten-point program. Along the way there have been wild
adventures and startling epiphanies, but there were also moments
of fear and inertia, cases of missteps and failure. The same applies
to the other people profiled in this book. But that's the true story
of how our lives are made. My hope is that you will see some of
yourself in these stories and will find in them some echo of your
own search—that these serendipitous lessons might provide a key
to answering the question that haunts all of us until we figure it
out: We've all made it this far. But now how do we make "making
it" matter?

Our work awaits.

The Work

1

. . . .

The Lesson of the Student

Come to Learn, Leave to Lead

"Flight attendants, please be seated and prepare for landing."

I sat back in my chair and started flipping through the British Airways magazine in my lap, hoping it would help pass the time before we touched down. As my eyes darted from one glossy picture to the next, I noticed that the young woman sitting to my right was gripping the armrest between us with a desperate ferocity, as if our safe landing were dependent on her hanging on to the support. She stared straight ahead, not blinking, not flinching. At one point she flicked her eyes in my direction and I gave her what I hoped was a reassuring smile, wanting to soothe her but not come off as weird. After a moment her face softened and she returned the smile. As if a trance had broken, her shoulders relaxed and the death grip she had on the armrest eased. She looked at me and said in an English accent, "I guess everything has changed."

I arrived at London's Heathrow Airport on September 23, 2001, on one of the first transatlantic flights granted airspace after the attacks of September 11, 2001. What should have been an unexceptional flight was filled with passengers afraid to sleep, instead sitting rigid and vigilant for the six-hour journey, like soldiers standing their post. I was right there with them, fighting off the idea that kept reappearing somewhere in my mind that this flight might be my last. I had just turned twenty-three.

The passengers applauded the crew as the plane touched down on the runway at Heathrow, a ritual likely shared on aircraft around the world that day, and we all collectively breathed a sigh of relief. This at first seemed odd to me, the idea of applauding someone for successfully accomplishing their job. Nobody applauds the garbage collector as they patrol a neighborhood collecting overstuffed bags filled with the week's trash. Nobody applauds the taxi driver as they pull to a stop and yank the receipt from the meter. But the repeated images emblazoned into our minds, planes that took off but never landed, reminded us of the miracle of landing. While I would later learn that in other countries, applause for a safe landing is a kind of ritual, that day at Heathrow the clapping was something different. I smiled again at my new British friend seated next to me as we headed together toward baggage claim. Her smile back was one of relief.

Along with thirty other passengers on that plane, I was headed to Oxford University, one of the oldest and most prestigious institutions of higher learning in the world, but my mind swirled with grief for the lives taken too soon.

Less than two weeks earlier, September 11, 2001, had been my little sister's twenty-first birthday. I was scheduled to have a meeting that day at Morgan Stanley, whose offices were in one of the towers, but I'd moved it to September 13 because my mother and I decided to surprise my sister for her birthday. Mom and I were in the car, driving up from Baltimore to New Jersey, where my sister lived, when we began to get the news. By the time the second tower fell, we knew we would never make it to New Jersey. Once we were able to confirm that my sister was safely at home, we turned around and drove home.

I'd done work, through the military, on the rise and ramifications of radical Islamism before September 11. I'd done research on South America's tri-border region, the lawless area between Argentina, Brazil, and Paraguay where Islamist terrorists were suspected to train, and I had closely followed the events around the suicide bombing of the USS *Cole* that killed seventeen American servicemen. I wasn't one of these people that had never heard of the group Al-Qaeda before. Still, I had no idea this was coming or what it was when it first went down. I was a reserve officer, not exactly privy to the National Security Council's daily briefing. But my years of military training told me this much: I knew that when the first reports came in from Washington saying "we are going to respond," that could only mean one thing: we were going to war.

When our plane landed in London on September 23, all of the passengers sat patiently and waited for the seat belt light to be turned off, then gratefully filed off the plane. Everyone was unusually polite and deferential—very different from the usual center-aisle mosh pit that forms when it's time to disembark. Our countries would soon be at war, but in the moments after the towers fell, there was this: small pockets of unprecedented peace.

This was the context in which I opened the next stage of my life. Part of me wondered if I was making the right choice. I was leaving behind my family and friends, including my mother. I was leaving behind my home country, which was still reeling from a terrorist attack, while starting a new life far away from the people whom I loved the most and who depended on me. I had an unbelievable opportunity in England, but I never felt more American than the moment I left it.

My American Journey was, not coincidentally, the name of one of the most influential books I'd ever read. When I was a teenager attending military school, few books offered me the opportunity to see myself—and my potential—the way Colin Powell's autobiography did. The book was published in the aftermath of the first war in Iraq, but before his beleaguered term as secretary of state, when he helped usher in the second Iraq War. When I read the book, my sense of politics was hazy at best, but what drew me to it were the stunning similarities between our early journeys.

Like me, Powell hailed from Jamaican roots. He was born in New York and I was born in Maryland, but we were both raised in the Bronx. We were both shaped by our military experience. My short time around the military—as a cadet in military school—had changed me. It gave me more discipline and direction, but more than that, it provided me with a kind of brotherhood that I had never imagined would be possible. I suspected the same was true for Powell, who had reached the highest rank the Army had to offer: a four-star general and chairman of the Joint Chiefs of Staff.

One big difference between us—aside from the fact that Powell was among the most famous people in the world and I was an anonymous teenager—was that Powell was a father, whereas I was a son. In his book, Powell tells of a letter he wrote each of his children when they turned sixteen. My own father was not alive and could not write me such a letter, so I took Powell's advice as if it had come from my own dad:

> You now begin to leave childhood behind and start on the road to manhood. . . . You will establish definitively the type person you will be the remaining fifty years of your lifetime. You know what is right and wrong and I have confidence in your judgment. Don't be afraid of failure. Be more afraid of not trying. . . . Take chances and risks—not foolhardy actions, but actions which could result in failure, yet promise success and reward. And always remember that no matter how bad something may seem, it will not be that bad tomorrow.

Don't be afraid of failure. Take chances and risks. Have confidence in your judgment. I thought of those words on the morning of September 23, 2001. To me the lesson in those words was that life will throw opportunities of all kinds at you—but it's up to you to use your judgment and *take the risks* of seizing the opportunities that make the most sense. The risk is that you might fail, but, as General Powell said, "no matter how bad something may seem, it won't be that bad tomorrow."

Just before I left for graduate school in England, I attended something the Rhodes Trust called "Bon Voyage Weekend," a chance for the newly selected Rhodes Scholars to meet their fellow scholars and learn more about the opportunities ahead; a time to celebrate, but also to find out the price of the ticket. As for the literal price, we were told that the bills for the two- or three-year adventure in Oxford, England, would be taken care of. Flights to and from the United States, covered. Travel expenses to see the world—as long as it had to do with our research—were expensed. Adults who were already changing the world rushed over to congratulate us for hardly doing much more than having good grades and potential. We were in our early twenties, most of us barely old enough to drink legally and still not old enough to handle our liquor, as we'd go on to prove nightly once we got to Oxford.

We listened intently as Admiral Stansfield Turner, former director of the CIA, and Joseph Nye, former chairman of the National Intelligence Council and father of the international relations theory of neoliberalism, spoke on how the Rhodes Scholarship helped to prepare them for careers spent shaping national security in our nation for a generation. We laughed as former senator (and NBA star) Bill Bradley shared comical stories about trying to fit his six-foot-seven-inch frame through Oxford's ancient doorways, built in a shorter age. We all rushed to take pictures with Bill Clinton, the former Rhodes Scholar who had just left the Oval Office after completing his twenty-four-year career in elected office.

But of course 9/11 had happened just two weeks earlier, and even amid the celebrations and camaraderie, the events of that day hung over everything. We were being inducted into a prestigious fellowship, but there was also a sense in which we were being enlisted into an urgent though undefined battle. This was underlined one night when we all sat quietly as we shared a meal with Solicitor General Ted Olson, a man who was still deep in mourning and who painfully recounted the story of the last phone conversation he had had with his wife, Barbara Olson, on board American Airlines Flight 77 en route to Los Angeles, a plane that had been flown instead into the Pentagon on 9/11. Once she realized the plane was being hijacked, she called her husband, unaware of the other two planes that had already flown into the World Trade Center in NYC. She called him to tell him the plane had just been commandeered; she wondered what she should do. Then the line went dead. The fact that Olson came to speak to us while still mourning the sudden death of his wife was a testament to how important he thought it was to send us off with a strong sense of duty to our country's new, undefined mission.

It was already clear, just from that weekend, that the Rhodes Trust was giving me access to a world that was pretty unrecognizable compared to anything I'd seen before. I felt overwhelmed and undeserving, the arbitrary recipient of a golden ticket to a secret world, a school so old it has no official founding date (records indicate that teaching at Oxford existed as early as 1096). When I told my friends back home about the fancy hotels and dinners and the VIPs who lined the walls of every room we entered, they listened and smiled with pride but weren't sure exactly what to say. I was disoriented and hoping that someone could help me make sense of it. And the most remarkable thing about this was that there was no catch. No hidden cameras recording it all as a social experiment, no small writing at the bottom of the contract, no unwritten rules we all would learn about the hard way. This was a world where they made only two requests of you. The first was clear and concise: to learn. This learning wasn't the same as the grade-grubbing that had defined so much of our academic lives to that point. In fact, for many of the classes I would take over there, pass/fail was standard. The mandate to learn simply meant to come back a different person than the person you were when you arrived. More deeply informed, more cultured, more prepared.

The second request was a bit more enigmatic. The scholarships were established in 1903 and outlined four criteria to be used in the selection of the scholars:

- Literary and scholastic attainments.
- Energy to use one's talents to the full.
- Truth, courage, devotion to duty, sympathy for and protection of the weak, kindliness, unselfishness, and fellowship.
- Moral force of character and instincts to lead, and to take an interest in one's fellow beings.

In his will, Cecil Rhodes stated distinctly that he wanted the scholars "to fight the world's fight." None of us were sure exactly what that meant. When a mentor of mine, Baltimore mayor Kurt Schmoke, first encouraged me to apply for the Rhodes Scholarship, he made it clear that he wanted me to know who Cecil Rhodes was before applying to accept his money. Mayor Schmoke, a brilliant and often radical black man—he famously pushed for decriminalization of drugs at the height of the drug-fueled epidemic of violence in Baltimore—walked me through the life and crimes of Rhodes. I hadn't known anything about Rhodes before that conversation, but since then I have never forgotten who he was.

Cecil Rhodes was born in 1853 in England, and made his name and fortune in southern Africa as one of the founders of the diamond mining company DeBeers. He died young, as one of the richest men in the world. He left a legacy of bold entrepreneurialism and aggressive wealth accumulation, but of course he's remembered for more than that. Cecil Rhodes was also a brutal and violent racist whose extreme tactics to control black labor and undermine black sovereignty went hand in hand with his unabashed belief in Anglo-Saxon supremacy.

Southern Africa, with its wealth and its vicious racism, was then in many ways a mirror of Rhodes. I had had a bit of personal experience with South Africa. As an undergraduate, I studied abroad in the townships outside of Johannesburg, where I got to see first-hand how black people still struggled to overcome the legacy of apartheid. I also had a connection through my grandfather, Papa Jim. In the 1960s, he had been appointed the first black minister in the more than three-hundred-year history of the Dutch Reformed Church, which was also the official religion of apartheid South Africa. He often told us about the racist death threats he received as his reward. After his appointment, church leaders asked him to lead a delegation of clergy to South Africa. Upon arriving in Johannesburg, he was informed by state security that the airport was as far as he would be allowed to go—he would not be permitted to leave the terminal. Eventually the party he was supposed to meet and stay with in South Africa had to come to him. They conducted their meeting in the airport terminal, where my grandfather prayed with them—for change, for hope, for unity, for forgiveness, for freedom. After that my grandfather promptly left that murderous regime and returned to America.

In my finalist interview for the scholarship, the name of Cecil Rhodes came up again. Steven Pfeiffer, the head of the selection committee in my region, sat across from me. A senior partner at one of the most well-respected law firms in the world, Fulbright and Jaworski, he looked every inch the success he was, with his tailored suit and chiseled leading-man features. He leaned forward, closing the distance between us, and said my name. My full name: Westley Watende Omari Moore. Then he paused—maybe for effect, maybe because he was thinking about how to best relay the question. In that moment of silence, everyone in the room leaned in a bit, as if he were sharing something special with each of us.

"Wes, you studied in South Africa and you saw firsthand the impact of the legacy of Cecil Rhodes. You are African American. How does it feel sitting here before us today and asking to receive his money?"

I hesitated before answering, replaying the question in my mind. *How* could I sit there and ask for this money to study despite knowing clearly where the money had come from? The money came from the bloodshed and lives lost in those toxic mines. It came from fathers, husbands, and sons who never returned to their families so that DeBeers could, at the time, control close to 90 percent of the world's diamond revenues. I also knew I was the *last* person Cecil Rhodes would have wanted his money going to. He despised me through the distance of the history that separated us, and didn't even know me. I thought for a moment more.

"I know all too clearly the legacy of Cecil Rhodes, and there are two reasons I feel not just comfortable but honored being in front of you today," I began. "The first reason is that I know Cecil Rhodes would be spinning in his grave if he knew that I was a finalist for his award."

There was some uncomfortable laughter around the table, accompanied by nods of agreement.

I continued, this time with more certainty, "The other reason is because I know how many people had to fight and die in order for me to be able to sit here in front of you. I don't consider this asking you for Cecil Rhodes's money, I consider this fulfilling a promise I made to the countless people who came before me to give me this opportunity."

I held my breath until Pfeiffer smiled. I looked around the table at the faces of the other board members, who, following Steven's lead, were now smiling at me. Hours later my name was being called as a member of the class of 2001 Rhodes Scholars. It was an honor that had particular resonance for my Jamaican-born family in the Bronx. It didn't matter to them that Bill Clinton had been a Rhodes Scholar or that George Stephanopoulos and Bill Bradley had been Rhodes Scholars, too. In my home, the most famous Rhodes Scholar was Michael Manley, the charismatic and iconic former prime minister of Jamaica. When the news arrived back home that I had been awarded a distinction shared by such a great man, my beloved grandparents suddenly understood the magnitude of the opportunity. My grandfather was a proud man, and showering praise or excessive emotion was not really his thing. If you did something remarkable, the most you could expect to get out of him was "very good job." But when I got to Michael Manley's name in the list of past recipients, I finally heard the excitement in his voice.

"Michael Manley!" he exclaimed, beaming. Over the next years Mama Win and Papa Jim never failed to make the connection for friends, family, and strangers alike. And they never asked me about the man from whom the fellowship took its name.

Over the course of our lives we all have opportunities, both large and small, to experience things that will bring us into new worlds and expand our boundaries beyond the familiar. This is never more true than when we're students, a time in our lives when people basically hurl opportunities at us—opportunities to learn, to meet new people, to be exposed to things we've never seen before.

Some of us—particularly those of us who grew up as immigrants, minorities, or outsiders because of race, class, sex, or any of a thousand other reasons—might hesitate when those opportunities come flying at us. Sometimes we think they're not for us, or that they were never meant for people who looked like us. Thought like us. Came from backgrounds like ours. We feel like imposters even being in the room. In psychology, this is known as the "impostor syndrome," a collection of feelings of inadequacy that persist even when evidence exists that the opposite is true. I don't want to minimize the power of that feeling; it can be crippling to gaze around a room where no one looks like you and still muster the nerve to act like you're entitled to everything on offer. I also learned—as when I sat for that Rhodes interview—that sometimes you feel like you're trying to participate in a system that's designed to exclude you or people like you. But if you've managed to make it into the room, whether it's a classroom, a boardroom, or the Situation Room at the White House, chances are that generations of people sacrificed for you to be there. And those doors generally don't open for just anyone. You don't deserve those opportunities as much as anyone; you may deserve them more than anyone. But more than that, you owe it to the people who came before you to seize them. And in taking advantage of the resources and opportunities that are available to us, we can also transform their intent and impact. I respected and embraced Cecil Rhodes's mandate for the scholars who would take his name—"to fight the world's fight." But I knew that my idea of the world's fight would be vastly different from his. Now I just had to figure out what, exactly, that fight would be.

■ ■ ■

We were met at the airport by Bob Wyllie, a gloriously friendly Englishman, rumpled and charming as a character on the old Benny Hill sitcoms my grandparents watched when I was a kid. He was the porter of Rhodes House, and eventually became a cherished friend. Rhodes House was the central meeting point for the Oxford students from around the world who were part of the Rhodes program.

A majestic building on its own, Rhodes House appeared modest in the sea of extravagance that surrounded it, glorious buildings that made the oldest structures in the United States seem newborn. Whenever you'd come by Rhodes House you knew the conversations would be stimulating, the alcohol would be free-flowing, and you'd be welcomed in by Bob's friendly face. The abundant alcohol certainly kept things interesting, but more than that, the conversations were different, more intense than anything I had experienced before. They straddled an odd balance of being less rushed but more urgent, strategically focused and frenetically ephemeral at the same time.

We did not have a formal mailing system at Oxford, just a pigeonhole where mail and announcements were left. This proudly archaic system was used primarily for announcements about lecture changes and college-wide parties, but when I first arrived at Wolfson College, my new Oxford home, my pigeonhole took on a different role: a place for complete strangers to share condolences. More than half a dozen letters, cards, and handwritten circulars were left by people I had yet to meet but who were aware I was from the United States and who wanted to express their sympathies. They didn't know whether or not I had been directly affected

by the tragedy of September 11, and they didn't care: they were
driven by the need to make clear that we stood arm in arm against
the attack. The messages were simple, moving expressions of our
shared humanity. It was a strange way to begin my time at Oxford,
but I welcomed it. The coming days would complicate those first,
earnest messages of sympathy.

I learned early that even if you did not drink, a prerequisite for
Oxford life was exploring the various watering holes around the
campuses. Pubs such as the Kings Arms and the Eagle and Child
became as familiar as the dozens of libraries that Oxford boasted,
and were the homes of freewheeling, passionate conversation. My
American accent was enough to prompt hours' worth of conversation with British and international students, who were in-
tensely curious about the details of the destruction, its emotional
aftermath, and the anticipated reaction of the Americans to the
attack—or, from the perspective of many I spoke with, anticipated
overreaction. I found myself in the uncomfortable position of
spokesperson for the United States. But my presumed expertise in
all things American drew all sorts of people to me, which allowed
me to hear the unfiltered points of view of Iranians, Spaniards,
Brazilians, Japanese, South Africans, Australians, and Egyptians, as
well as my fellow American students, in an environment where
everyone felt safe to share, vent, and challenge. In time, the conversations went beyond 9/11. I had conversations with an American
Air Force officer about whether we should forgive Osama bin
Laden, to send a larger message to the world about our capacity for
benevolence. I talked about animal rights with a Belgian student
who wanted to shut down the science labs to free the chimpanzees
that were being used in experiments. And I remember an almost
prophetic conversation with Matías, an outspoken Argentinean

economics major, who reminded me of a grimmer, more intense, Latin Woody Allen. We were talking about the upcoming global clash over the inherent inequality of the capitalist system.

"You will see, my friend," he said, hand wrapped around a tepid beer, "we cannot have continued disparity and an appeased underclass. Not just in the developing world, but in the developed world."

I was slightly intimidated by his accented English and cosmopolitan air, the kind of sophistication that only a tweedy twentysomething in a dinner jacket can confidently pull off, but to me his predictions seemed improbable. I'd been to shantytowns in southern Africa that made the worst of American poverty seem like a life of absolute decadence, and even there, the post-apartheid regime had not been shaken by riots over scarcity or wealth disparity. Given that, I couldn't imagine Americans or Brits, with their high standards of living, rising up over income inequality.

He scoffed at my disagreement. "I respect your Western arrogance and bias," he said with as much sarcasm as the seriousness of our conversation could bear. "But when someone feels as though they are relegated to the permanent underclass, it's difficult to ask them to keep it in perspective."

I'd never been accused of Western arrogance before. Back at Johns Hopkins, I usually played the role of the skeptic, pointing out the biased presumptions of my classmates from more privileged backgrounds. I wasn't quite sure how to wear the accusation of privilege directed at me. And, of course, Matías turned out to be right. Within a decade, not only would we see "people power" overthrow long-standing regimes in the Middle East, but we'd see massive street protests in modernizing Brazil, anti-austerity riots all over Western Europe including the United Kingdom, and in the United States a month-long occupation in New York's financial district. And, yes, even in South Africa, strikes over working conditions and wages turned into violent clashes with the government. In 2001 it was hard for me and many others to see that conflict wouldn't just be geopolitical but would attack basic political and economic systems from within. But for people whose angles on the world were different from mine, it was easier to see. This was the second layer of my Oxford education, and it occurred not in a classroom but over the intoxicated glaze of warm beer and bangers and mash, listening to people with wildly varied accents explaining their perspective of the world to me, and me testing my own beliefs against them.

Our course work almost seemed secondary. I studied international relations, and in my first year spent much of the time focusing on pre–World War I conflict and the economic implications of post–World War I recovery. We learned from world-renowned professors who had been using the same lesson plans for decades. It was all interesting, but it was not lost on anyone in my class that these tried and familiar lectures didn't necessarily help us map the world we lived in now, one that was about to enter its own war through a cloud of uncertainty. The only thing clear about the war to come was that it was coming.

I had been an officer in the United States Army since 1998. After I graduated from Valley Forge Military College, I received a commission to become a second lieutenant. When I was commissioned, we were a nation in a state of relative peace. Most of my fellow soldiers joined the military because of two seeming assurances: (1) they could get their schooling paid for, and (2) they would not see combat. Well, at least we would still get our schooling paid for. Soldiers I had trained with and served with were now preparing for combat—desert training, drills on dealing with chemical weapon attacks, and, of course, preparing for the ritual of leaving home and family with no promise of return. I was distracted with thoughts of my old comrades and their new reality on the other side of an ocean, while I was at Oxford learning about the assassination of Archduke Franz Ferdinand and how to distinguish between after-dinner ports. The world was spinning faster, yet in Oxford we were sitting in sixteenth-century buildings trying to slow it down enough to understand it.

While I might not have had many classmates who shared my skin color and experience, history gave me more than a few templates for how best to use some of the opportunities being thrown my way. I read about the great African American poet Langston Hughes, for instance, and took some inspiration from him. In 1932 he sailed to the Soviet Union, thus beginning a series of journeys that are chronicled in his book *I Wonder as I Wander*. Throughout the Depression, as the world fell apart and opportunities that once seemed abundant disappeared, Hughes used travel as fuel for his curiosity, fodder for his creativity, and balm for his weary soul. During the same era, when black men were being hung from trees for even looking at a white woman, Hughes bravely and boldly traveled to not only Russia (where he spent a year) but also Cuba, Haiti, Central Asia, Japan, and Spain, which was in the midst of a civil war.

Closer to home, I also considered the life of my grandfather. Despite the occasional hostility of his co-religionists—and his own lack of financial resources—he never stopped traveling the world. He was born in South Carolina, but he was so young when his family moved away that he had no memory of his experiences there, though he knew the stories well. While he was still a child, the Ku Klux Klan let his family know they were not welcome and ran them not only out of town but out of the country—all the way to Jamaica. They left the United States as heartbroken exiles from a place they loved but which didn't extend that love back to them. My grandfather always knew, deep down, that he would one day return to his place of birth. From afar, he believed in the American dream, even if his earliest understanding of the nation conveyed a clear message that his family, my family, were not part of the dream.

He began his travels when he and my grandmother moved from Jamaica to the United States so that he could attend Lincoln University, a historically black college in Pennsylvania, where he received his degree. Once he was appointed a minister, he followed his theological obligations and humanistic inclinations by working for people in need all over the world: victims of tsunamis in Southeast Asia, sufferers of famine in East Africa, survivors of attempted genocide in Eastern Europe. It was from him that I first learned the power of a passport.

Once I got settled in at Oxford, I found every possible excuse to travel. My course work was flexible; the course of study I chose meant we never had consistent exams, only regular readings and discussions. And the academic calendar left plenty of unoccupied space in the school year. I understood that my perspective was still being formed. Oxford would give me the tools to help shape and articulate it, but the world itself was the raw material I would apply it to.

London was a great jumping-off point for almost anywhere in

the world. Airline competition led to cheap travel options, simple geography meant you could get around Europe, Africa, and Asia with relative ease, and stipend money from the scholarship meant I had a green light to see the world without worrying about going into the red.

For my master's thesis, I had chosen to research the rise and ramifications of radical Islamism in the Western Hemisphere, a subject that had new relevance and importance in light of the recent attacks, and which also justified my extraordinary travel schedule. When I was in the U.S. Army Reserve while finishing college in Baltimore, I first heard about groups such as Al-Qaeda, Hamas, the Taliban, and Hezbollah. Prior to the attacks of 9/11, I would talk to people I knew about these issues, but their response was always distant and disconnected. "That sounds so interesting . . . ," was what I usually heard, mostly as a polite transition to the next topic of conversation.

Almost overnight I watched my niche research area become the entire world's urgent concern. My next stage of research couldn't be done in libraries; the subject was too new and nebulous. It required being out in the field. So I hung out at mosques in southern Lebanon, spoke with government officials and shopkeepers in Syria, smoked hookah pipes with young revolutionaries in Cairo, and traveled down to Foz de Iguazu with a former Argentinean intelligence officer. I grew out the hair on top of my head (back when I had hair on top of my head), let a patchy beard sprout on my face, grabbed my passport, and went. I tried to be a silent chameleon, watching subjects, movements, and tendencies. I tried to fit in, despite my former college football player's frame, the oddness of being a black man in some of the areas I visited, and the occasional Baltimore twang inflecting my broken Spanish or Arabic. But my life experience served me surprisingly well in these new environments.

This is what I've come to think of as the code-switching bonus—a reluctant survival tactic for a kid from the Bronx or Baltimore turned into a life skill. Code-switching is a kind of cultural multilingualism that is a particular specialty of minorities who find themselves immersed in the majority culture. Throughout my life, I found myself trying to fit in and making whatever adjustments I needed so that I didn't stick out needlessly in a given environment. When my mother sent me across town to a private school because our neighborhood school was too dangerous, for instance, I figured out to make sure my Bronx persona—the language, demeanor, confidence—would fall away as my train pulled into the station next to my private school. I was like a comedian about to start a new impression: with a turn, my face would change. Suddenly I smiled more, not because I was happier, but because I wanted to seem less threatening and intimidating to the kids around me.

Code-switching is something that most of us begin to do unconsciously. Usually it's pointed out for us by others; say, a friend from the old neighborhood sees us in our new environment and is startled to hear changes in our tone and vocabulary or see our body language change. When we first notice it in ourselves, we can be startled, too, and disappointed or resentful. But then we realize it's a tool as useful as speaking a second language, as long as we use it not out of shame or embarrassment but strategically, as a way to reach out to people or accomplish other goals. It's a skill I honed at every step of my life—in middle school in the Bronx, in military school in suburban Philadelphia, Pennsylvania, at military assignments in places such as Fort Benning in rural Georgia. I had mastered the art of fine-tuning my persona according to the needs of the situation—in this case, as I traveled through the Arab world as a tall, black American, the need was to blend in and learn, and to make my subjects feel like they were not subjects at all.

My research caught the attention of my Oxford professors, many of whom found it almost comical that this six-foot-two American army officer believed that a scraggly beard was enough to go unrecognizable in the circles I was hoping to penetrate. It also caught the attention of the U.S. government.

The Oxford winters can be dreary and wet but are not generally cold enough for snow. If you are not prepared or particularly adaptable, those winters have been known to color the entire experience. One day I sat in my well-designed Oxford efficiency at Wolfson College, a room so small that I ate, slept, brushed my teeth, and studied without ever having to take more than two steps in any direction. My cell phone began to ring, with a distinctive double ring indicating that the call was from overseas. My caller ID flashed an enigmatic "unknown."

I answered and heard the voice of Michael Fenzel, then a major in the U.S. Army and a good friend and mentor. I had met Mike a year earlier after an introduction from the head football coach at Johns Hopkins, Jim Margraff. Coach Margraff knew none of us on the Hopkins squad were going to be playing in the NFL—we practiced, played hard, and were successful, but our Division III school's stands were not exactly filled with pro scouts. But Coach made it his purpose to develop us not simply as athletes but also as men. When I was a senior, Coach Margraff called up one of his former linebackers to talk to me. Mike Fenzel was no longer stalking quarterbacks; instead, he was now a three-time combat veteran and infantry officer. Mike also had just received the White House

Fellowship and was working at the National Security Council as the director for transnational threats, a job whose title didn't properly capture its importance. Mike was in the Situation Room with the national security advisor, Condoleezza Rice, as the World Trade Center collapsed, and he was a member of the National Security Agency team that had to draw up an American response.

I was excited to get a call from Mike, but he wasn't just checking in. There was a clear reason for this call, and Mike was direct.

"Wes, I am going to put you in touch with Richard Falkenrath, Chris Hornbarger, and Pancho Kinney. You need to work for the Office of Homeland Security this summer."

The Office of Homeland Security, the precursor to the Department of Homeland Security, was created just months after the attacks of 9/11. Run by former marine and former governor of Pennsylvania Tom Ridge, the agency's difficult mission was to consolidate the nation's capabilities for responding to and preventing another domestic attack. Because of the research that had consumed me at Oxford, Mike felt I could help. He also felt I could learn. This was a chance to work on important issues—issues of war and peace—as they were being debated at the highest levels. Mike was inviting me on a path into that room. As Mike explained to me what the work would entail, his tone made it clear that this wasn't a request or suggestion. "No" was not an option. I wouldn't have said no, anyway. The only risk was failure.

As soon as the academic semester at Oxford ended, I was on my way to Washington, D.C.

THE WORKER #1

■ ■ ■ ■ ■ ■ ■ ■ ■ ■ ■ ■ ■ ■ ■ ■ ■

The Outsider

DANIEL LUBETZKY
CEO, KIND LLC

Some have labeled award-winning social entrepreneur Daniel
Lubetzky's quest for a two-state Israeli-Palestinian peace solution "quixotic." But even doubters acknowledge his genius. He's
harnessed capitalism to pursue and encourage economic justice and political-social bridge building around the world. For
him the label "outsider" is a badge of honor; he takes it to mean
that he possesses useful knowledge that hasn't reached the
mainstream. The other gift of being an outsider is that we can
take what we learn from the mainstream—take those resources
they have, resources that often, as in the case of Cecil Rhodes,
were stolen from other people at some point in history—and
bring them back to wherever we come from, to solve the problems that mean the most to us.

Meeting Daniel and speaking with him about these issues is to watch a man on fire. His quest for peace and social justice is powerful and persuasive. Here is Daniel's story.

The exponential growth of KIND bars, the health bar that rocketed from obscurity in 2003 to become the dream snack of foodies with a conscience, is nothing short of remarkable. The ingredients are serious nutrition, fabulous natural flavors (nothing in them you can't pronounce, the company promises), and heavy doses of good will, social justice, and kindness. And the name is no accident. In 2010, KIND started an interactive platform, which helps turn individual acts of kindness into a social movement. Through the platform, people can turn small acts of kindness into large-scale acts that give back to the world in a much bigger way. Every month, KIND invites its community to sign up for a KINDING mission—for instance, writing a thank-you note to someone in your life who has always had your back. If enough people participate in the mission, then KIND matches the spirit of that effort at a larger scale. So thank-you notes become care packages KIND donates to wounded vets. Among KIND's featured areas of giving are issues important to women, children, people living in poverty, and the chronically ill and hospitalized, as well as the environment.

So much good fosters a lot of company pride. "We've already inspired over twenty thousand acts of kindness and hit communities across the country," explains a beaming Adeena Cohen, who moved into KIND's marketing division after starting as Daniel's assistant. "Daniel's involved in developing the concept and being true to the brand's philosophy. Around here, we say 'and' instead of 'or': economically sustainable *and* socially impactful, healthy *and* tasty. I think what you really feel at KIND is it's not one or the other. People aren't working to create just financial success or to feel good. They're working for both. The social component attracts great talent. It's fun to work with people on this team, people who really care about more than themselves."

Daniel was born in 1968 into a small enclave of Jews living in a wealthy suburb of Mexico City, a place he describes as a "tightly and closely knit community, not apt to be open. Most of my friends were just friends among themselves." But that insularity rankled Daniel even as a boy. He was genetically programmed for a gregariousness that broke the boundaries of sameness.

Both of Daniel's parents, each with a history of growing up the "other," encouraged Daniel to explore the world outside the protected shell they created for their children. Though they chose to raise a family within the confines of a fairly closed community, both Roman and Sonia actively "made sure I had Christian friends," Daniel recalls. "Most of the friends I went to school with from when I was four until we left [for San Antonio, Texas] were Jewish. My mom had friends who were Christian. My parents enrolled me in classes and after-school programs so I'd develop friendships with kids who were different from me," he says in his still heavily accented English.

He pauses, then says quickly, as if to set the record straight about what his success means in the bigger picture, "I've always been the outsider. I've always done well as an outsider. I guess I like to celebrate differences and point out that I'm a very idiosyncratic thinker. I question things. It's about not accepting things as you're told, but asking why. I guess coming from that vantage helps me connect with other cultures and celebrate them."

Family had a big influence on him: "Without any doubt, my biggest influences are my dad and my mother. Whatever room my dad walked into, he emitted light and caring. He made everyone smile. The president of a bank or a bank clerk—didn't matter. People were touched by my dad. Not just people who were great friends, but people who he met in life and didn't assume he'd be so connected with them, so indelibly etched in their memory. That was my dad's personality and approach to humanity. To some degree, part of what shaped me was his warm and sweet nature, but maybe also the sense of persecution that made him feel he needed to build bridges."

Daniel knows that without the boomerang effect of kindness, he might not even be alive today: "When World War II was starting, Nazis and Lithuanian people started killing Jews. My dad came home one day with his father, and the superintendent of the building stopped them from heading upstairs. He led them to the garage. There was like this red liquid flowing through the door, covering the floor. And then they opened the garage door. They saw all these dead bodies, one on top of the other—all the Jewish tenants in the building where my dad and his family lived."

Daniel stops for a minute, the full impact of the horror-filled story hitting hard. Then he says, "The superintendent told my father, 'When they came they asked me to point out all the Jews. I did. And this is what happened to them. But I spared you because you treated me with respect. You looked me in the eye. So I spared you. Now go get your stuff and get out of here.' That was the circumstance in which they went back to the apartment and packed up everything they could. My grandfather, my father, his brother, and my grandmother moved to the ghetto."

The urge to close the divides, to see and evince the core goodness in everyone, stems in large measure from knowing what happened to his father and watching his father handle the trauma with grace. "This guy who spared my father and grandfather? He wasn't the sweetest guy. He pointed out all the other Jews in the building. I think my dad drew lessons from that about treating people with dignity. Even I drew lessons. I was impacted by his experience."

He remembers his mother's dismay whenever his father talked about the past. "'Roman,' my mother would say, 'why tell the kids these stories?' My dad would say, 'Sonia, they have to hear about it. I had to *live* through it.'"

His Mexican-born mother told Daniel that while she never denied her Jewishness, she did not discuss it unless asked directly. "She was the only Jewish kid in a cattle town in Mexican countryside. The way she handled it, we'd be in a taxi and the driver would make comments about Jews. People in Mexico don't assume you're Jewish because there are so few. Anyway, she'd try to reason with the driver, but from the perspective of a Christian. She'd try to encourage openness. It was surprising and shocking to listen to as a little kid. Then I started understanding. If the driver didn't know she was Jewish, maybe that would give her more credibility. I followed her advice when I was in those circumstances for a period of time," he acknowledges. "Now I make an explicit point of it even if it makes people uncomfortable."

The thing is, Daniel says, his mother is extraordinarily friendly. "She'll make friends with anybody at any point—waiting in line, in an elevator, in places where you least expect it. My mom and dad never had a problem to share popcorn with the people behind them in the movies or to stretch out a hand. That informed my personality."

That personality, says Daniel, is what's kept him from experiencing discrimination in any personal way. "To the extent I was exposed to it, it was so insignificant—as a Jew or Mexican. I do notice how there is latent anti-Semitism and prejudice against Latinos. I happen to have the personality and luxury of never having experienced direct discrimination. But I see it happening to others all the time."

And there is his latent fear that what happened yesterday can happen tomorrow. For him, every individual has the responsibility to be "ambassadors for our communities—Jews or Mexicans or whatever."

But fear of persecution isn't what drives him. It's his philosophy of determination. "I think I can change the world, and I can choose how to shape my life, to shape the community I live in."

This doesn't mean he's an optimist. People tend to confuse determination and positive attitude with false optimism or naiveté.

"You know how people say the glass is half empty or half full? Well, I've never seen it that way. The glass is at the middle level, but what are we going to do to fill it up? It's about whether you have an attitude that makes you do something. If you're not going to get off the couch, it doesn't make a difference. Optimism or pessimism can drive action. When I'm worried about the conflict in the Middle East getting worse, it drives me to do something."

As a teen, Lubetzky was making friends and decoding Texas subculture; he started buying watches and trinkets to sell on the flea market circuit. That morphed into a stall in a mall that rapidly became several stalls in multiple malls. He had as many as twenty college students on rotating shifts to man the booths. "Omigod, I had fun. What I love is creating new stuff. The money is way secondary. It's not what drives me. It's the challenge of building and creating something."

Fluently multilingual (he speaks Hebrew, French, Yiddish, English, and Spanish) and well practiced in decoding the "other," he moved easily in different circles. While studying abroad in the Middle East, he developed friendships with Israelis and Palestinians and began to ponder solutions to the seemingly unending struggle.

His intense intelligence took him to the top schools in the world, finishing with Stanford Law School and leading to jobs at top law firms and international consulting houses such as Sullivan and Cromwell and McKinsey and Company, but it was not until a trip to Israel that his passion for social change and social entrepreneurship merged. While there, he tasted for the first time a sun-dried tomato product that stopped him in his tracks. "I still remember that taste, but more important, the feeling," he says. Why couldn't he come up with a product that was this delicious, but which would also lead the way to communication and cooperation in the region that birthed that delicious tomato?

That was the birth of Peace Works LLC, a for-profit brand that measures success on much broader parameters than simply revenue growth. Peace Works brings together "neighbors" on opposing sides of political and/or armed conflicts to strategize and execute cooperative for-profit business plans focused on healthy food products. Peace Works buys for export. The theory: when destinies are linked in mutually beneficial enterprises, the common interest inspires trust and respect, perhaps paving the way for peace between rivals. Five percent of Peace Works profits go to the Peace Works Foundation. The foundation, in turn, supports a collection of initiatives, including One Voice, a grassroots movement to help mainstream, moderate Israelis and Palestinians wrest control from radicals and steer the campaign for reconciliation and coexistence.

One of the business platforms that exists under Peace Works LLC is Maiyet, a purveyor of luxury clothing and accessories (a pleated tank top runs $495, a pair of women's shoes about $900) that sources from master artisans in places such as Colombia, India, Indonesia, Italy, Kenya, Mongolia, and Peru. The company deploys customized training programs that allow its partners to create high-quality products, cultivate artisan businesses, encourage entrepreneurship, and forge paths to sustainable individual and community economic growth. Lubetzky is a cofounder.

The other major platform, KIND, has him fully engrossed at the moment. He is sampling a new bar flavor that will soon be released. He looks up and says with a smile, "I like this one—not too sweet." He is proud of his team and his work. He realizes that his training was solid and his execution is certain. We walk around his office meeting employees. I ask him about how the new flavors will impact the monetary growth of the company. He looks at me with his piercing blue eyes. "I don't want to talk profitability. Let's talk about impact."

2

．．．．．．．．．．

The Lesson of the Professional

The Wisdom of Quitting

My internship with the Department of Homeland Security would be unpaid, a far cry from the investment banking and consulting jobs many of my Oxford friends would be cashing in on during the summer. But it was good work. I'd be working with a group that was still undefined but had a mandate weightier than any I had ever assumed. Some of the people I'd be working with were famous—or at least Washington famous—and some worked in the shadows. Most intriguing for me, I would have the chance to see if my research into radical Islam could actually contribute something to this terrifying, fascinating, horrific moment.

We worked countless hours analyzing data, preparing position papers, and trying to map out what security meant in the post-9/11 world. Days came and went, and my internship, which lasted three months, seemed to flash by in an instant. The experience of interning at the Office of Homeland Security helped me realize something new about government. At its heart, the essence of government is *budgets*. You can tell what people value by how they spend their money, and government is no different. Anyone who works in policy has to understand budgets and how they work. The deeper I got into my internship and the more we discussed the intricacies of combining twenty-eight federal agencies to create this massive Department of Homeland Security (with over two hundred thousand employees), the more I realized how woefully unprepared I was to contribute to the conversation. I had a rudimentary understanding of the implications of policy, but trying to figure out how to plan and execute policy exposed my inexperience.

July 4, 2002. By the time the sun rose we were hunkered down at our desks putting the final touches on a plan that Governor Tom Ridge, who'd been tapped by President Bush to be the first director of homeland security, would be presenting to the president a week later. The sun beamed down through the humid air of Washington, D.C., that day with an intensity that everyone in the office noticed but nobody mentioned. We took the sweltering as a meteorological manifestation of the intensity of the work we were doing. It would almost have been odd to be doing the work in comfort.

At around eleven that morning our office door opened and the assertive voice of Governor Ridge boomed over my shoulder.

"How's my team doing?"

We perked up. We were tired, but upon hearing his voice we all reflexively sat up a little straighter. When I turned around I saw him standing there in his dark suit, sweating already from the Washington humidity, the perspiration adding a glow to his smiling face. He called all of us together and said, "I am with the president all day, but I wanted to stop by and let you know how much I appreciate the work you are doing. There are plenty of places you could be right now, but you are giving yourselves to serve a greater cause, a great cause, and our nation could not be more thankful."

Our first Independence Day since 9/11 was a big deal, in terms of both ceremony and security. People were scared that terrorists would take this national holiday as an opportunity to send a message. The president and his team, including Governor Ridge, made it a point to be visible to the public, to let it be known they would not cower or hide. They were seemingly everywhere that day, their schedules packed with more public events than usual. But the fact that Governor Ridge made it a point to also stop by the office and let us know he appreciated our work meant a great deal. And he also came bearing gifts.

"I know you cannot spend the day with your families cooking up food," he said, "so I brought some to you."

With that, a group of caterers walked into the open-plan office with platters of hot dogs and hamburgers and enough cold drinks to help us forget about the miasma of heat that engulfed us. We met the end of the speech—and the simultaneous arrival of the hot dogs—with applause. We gobbled down our American cuisine and toasted Independence Day with bottled water. And then we got back to work.

I returned to Oxford in the fall convinced that I had discovered my calling: I wanted to work in policy. I still didn't know exactly what that looked like or how to get the skills I need to achieve competency. But I was completely engaged in Washington, and inspired to see that bureaucrats were not necessarily the automatons that word usually conjures up. Under the circumstances we were in, given the crises we were confronting, the people who did the work of implementing policy were actually the behind-the-scenes heroes of government. Things were escalating all over. Soldiers, sailors, airmen, and marines now filled the caverns of mountainous eastern Afghanistan, and tens of thousands more began staging in the countries neighboring Iraq to begin operations in that country. The urgency was real. The number of world leaders who made pilgrimages to Oxford reminded us of this.

Every now and then, while part of my brain was speeding along making big plans to work at the center of policy and power in Washington, there was another part that kept asking, *Are you serious? Wes Moore, what are you doing here?* The more I kept saying yes to opportunities, the louder and louder that voice got. I couldn't shake the feeling of being a stranger in a strange land, whether I was in Washington or at Oxford.

Of course, I was still trying to follow the code imprinted on me by Colin Powell's book when I was a teenager: *take risks.* And I was excited about all of the revelatory and life-changing opportunities suddenly opening up to me. But this new world also felt adopted and distinct from what I still thought of as my true life. This is when I learned that the downside of too much code-switching is the occasional identity crisis. And it was starting to kick in for me. I felt the way I had the first time I met my girlfriend's parents: I tried hard to maintain my cool, but my internal temperature was rising by the moment, impatient for the moment when I could get away from their glare. I felt like I'd had a pretty good run, a very unexpected journey, but that I was running out of runway.

There are a few tried-and-true paths for many of the young people who are lucky enough to earn the title of Rhodes Scholar.

Seemingly days after students receive their course schedules, they also receive welcome boxes full of swag from McKinsey, Boston Consulting Group, Goldman Sachs, and other financial and consulting firms that recruit students like birds of prey scanning the savannah for dinner. The students who end up taking the well-trodden path to the cobblestones of Wall Street or the oversized glass doors of international consulting firms are often remarkable individuals. It's easy to think of them as craven, greedy, narrow-minded future masters of the universe. But that's unfair. Members of my class had literally discovered the cure to diseases before walking across the stage to receive their undergraduate diploma. We had a legally blind mathematics and computer science double major who committed himself to working for disabled Costa Ricans. One of my classmates was a musical director who by the age of twenty-one was touring the world with his original compositions. Another friend's experiences included extensive paleontological digs in the Sahara, where he helped discover three new species of dinosaurs and other fossils that rewrote the history of Africa during the Cretaceous. But the flip side of all this prodigious achievement was the possibility that we'd peaked early. We'd all heard the unwelcome joke that a Rhodes Scholar is "someone who had a wonderful career behind them." These were some of the most interesting, engaging, and compelling people I had ever met or ever would meet. And many of them were heading to Wall Street.

I don't mean to diminish that choice. Some entered careers as consultants or in finance because they'd truly found their passion. Many of them entered with the very real intention of "doing this for a few years"—making money, learning, seeing the world (or at least the variety of high-end office spaces around the world)—and then transitioning to their true calling. But we know how that movie ends. Comfort sets in. Schools get expensive. Car prices rise. Second homes have mortgages that need to be covered. The golden handcuffs start to pinch.

There's a great passage in a recent novel, *In the Light of What We Know,* in which the narrator, a former Oxford student from Pakistan, describes his wife's evolution over the years:

> When I met her, she had come to finance after a year of teaching in a school in a Kenyan township near Kisumu, by Lake Victoria . . . she would tell me how she wanted to go back and spend more time there, that she was going to squirrel away her earnings in finance for the freedom to do so soon . . . But fifteen years later, with her idealism faded, she approached finance with the zeal of a convert. The last time our conversation alighted on the topic of her days in Africa, of her dreams then, I caught in her eye the look of embarrassment.

So many of my fellow students never left those offices in the end. How we spend our days is how we spend our lives, and it's the rare person who can walk away from what feels like a sure thing.

After my experience in Washington the summer before, I realized how much I wanted to be involved in policy, but after my experience with budgets and budgeting, I also realized how woefully ill equipped I was when it came to understanding the intricacies of finance. That was the sort of thing I'd need to master if I wanted to turn my passion for policy into a profession. I was also still feeling profoundly unsure of myself. What good could I do in Washington when I didn't yet have a feel for the sort of financial thinking that budget work requires? What good could I do anywhere? How would I earn back the investment my family put into me?

As I came to the end of my second year at Oxford, I was full of anxiety about my next move. In moments of doubt, I always turn to the friends and mentors I've accumulated throughout my academic life. It's incredibly valuable to have this network, and I haven't done much to gain it aside from showing up at school. This is one of the real values of school—and, in my opinion, one of the incentives missing when we pitch higher education to kids who aren't sure about it. School isn't just a place to learn; it's a place to meet really smart people who can help you in ways you can't even predict. One of those people in my life was Chris Ogeneski, the wide receiver coach at Johns Hopkins—he was only a decade removed from running patterns as a Johns Hopkins receiver himself. He had a "Clark Kent" image among the players, because by day he was a high-flying derivatives trader for Deutsche Bank, one of the largest banks in the world. But as soon as the markets closed, when most traders were heading home or directly to the nearest bar, Coach Ogs, as we affectionately called him, was heading to Homewood Field to teach receivers how to create separation with cornerbacks and catch the ball at its highest point. He was passionate about football and about teaching. Trading was a day job that paid him more than handsomely. But coaching is what he loved.

In my season of indecision, I made the trip back to Baltimore to see him, while also hoping that the warm embrace of home would add a sense of clarity. I sat with Coach Ogs in the Papermoon Café, a quirky diner in the Hamden section of Baltimore known as much for its Technicolor decor as for its crab omelets and twenty-four-hour service.

"What would you like, hon?" the waitress asked me in her distinct Baltimore twang.

I wanted to say, *Life advice, please,* but decided on shrimp and grits.

As we waited for our food, Coach asked in his matter-of-fact way what was going on, and I shared my uncertainty about my next step. I told him how I wanted to be involved in policy and public service, but that when I stared at spreadsheets the numbers all blurred together. I asked him about business school, or maybe law school, and probably about fifteen other options.

He told me it was obvious that I needed some training, but grad school would be a bad idea. Coach was in a lot of ways a practical man, and he told me that I could learn what I needed while working in the business world. He offered to make some introductions.

And with that, I joined the parade of my classmates into finance. *I'll only do this a few years,* I thought. In the back of my mind I heard the rattle of expensive handcuffs.

"Let's head to the Babble City!"

Zach led the caravan of banking analysts and associates who were on their way to the pub closest to Deutsche Bank's main offices on London's Liverpool Street. After months of working on a single deal, including one last all-nighter the night before it closed, we could finally take a breather. Some of us were smart enough to go home and sleep; some decided that heading home to see their families, who they saw far too little of, made the most sense. But those of us who had no family responsibilities and who made too much money for the little time we had to spend it made a beeline to the pub to do what we did best. Credit cards were drawn from our wallets like swords leaving their sheaths. It was time to celebrate.

I was now in my second year of working in investment banking in London. I joined Deutsche Bank right after I completed my studies at Oxford, and while both were in England, one could not have been further from the other. Oxford prided itself on patience, reflection, and deliberation, every conclusion arrived at after what seemed like eons of debate. The world of banking was its antithesis, an industry built on adrenaline and decisiveness. It was a place where traders made trades as fast as their computers would allow them, a place where tweedy thoughtfulness was less valued than keyboard cowboys with an all-chips-in swagger.

The deal we'd completed, which eventually became known as the Aires Deal, was certainly one worth celebrating for a young banker. At the time it was the largest deal of its type, a debt deal where Germany repackaged 5 billion euros (at the time the equivalent of $8.5 billion) in bilateral loans to Russia.

Governments can really only make money two ways: through taxes or through debt issuance. Selling debt allows the general public to fund government expenditures in exchange for an expected profit—it's how governments get access to the cash they need to run their operations. These deals can't be done by the governments themselves, so banks are irreplaceable in the process, for better or for worse. Deutsche Bank was co-lead on the deal, and I was the junior associate, which meant that all of the grunt work fell on my shoulders. We ran the numbers so many times we almost had them memorized. We put together graphs and charts that would be used by the German government. We were told by our directors and managing directors that we would be part of history once this deal closed. So I joined in with my smiling comrades to celebrate, but my smiles hid a deeper agnosticism about the whole thing. We were told to be proud of what had just happened, but I didn't feel any real sense of accomplishment.

I remember speaking with my grandmother Mama Win not long before. As a public school teacher in the South Bronx, Mama Win worked from sunup to sundown, taking care of the home and working hard outside of it. It wasn't lost on me that in my first year in banking I was making more money than my grandmother probably made over half of her entire career. I had no skills and no experience, just a degree and a new corporate credit card. My hours were long, but I didn't end many of them feeling a genuine sense of fulfillment. I felt privileged to be where I was, but this was not the fulfillment of a dream, because I had never dreamed about this life. It wasn't because I had some long-standing problem with finance, but because I hadn't even known there were jobs like this to dream about. Nobody in my family had. Now I wasn't just peering into a new world but living in it. There was a seat at the table with my name on it. I was learning about budgets, spreadsheets, and how governments financed themselves, just as I'd planned. But nothing about it felt real.

Nothing, that is, except the pride my family felt in my success. They didn't really have any idea of how well I was doing financially. And they didn't care. The source of their pride and happiness never stemmed from that. They simply knew that fifty years earlier they'd come to the United States from Jamaica with only a vague concept of this American dream everyone talked about. Their embrace of the American dream was even more remarkable because of my grandfather's painful history with this country. So what was this American dream to them? They looked at where my sisters and I stood now, our opportunities and our cushier lifestyles, and all the sacrifices they had made seemed well worth it. And it was with that that my grandparents began to understand what the American Dream meant to them. This "dream" was not simply about the new opportunities that this country can afford you, but the happiness of watching your children and grandchildren and great-grandchildren accomplish things that would've been impossible for you. It's watching with joy your sacrifices manifest in your loved ones living out their lives in peace and with unbridled opportunity. My success, such as it was, was their confirmation.

One day while I was spending a month in New York working on a deal, I took the forty-minute subway ride up to the Bronx. The subway system in New York is amazingly efficient at showing off the jarring disparities between neighborhoods—one ride can bring you from the underbelly of poverty to the pinnacle of affluence, all for the price of a cup of coffee. I'd learned the route by heart. The number 2 train took me directly from my office on Wall Street to my grandparents' house off Gun Hill Road in the Bronx. The train rolled beneath the towering buildings of lower Manhattan, the neon lights of midtown, the urban suburbia of the Upper West Side, and the teeming street life of Harlem. Forty minutes after leaving an odorless, glass-sheathed downtown monolith, my nose was filled with the smell of oxtail and pigs' feet as I walked into my grandparents' Bronx home. Some folks would literally turn their noses up at our family's choice of cuisine, but for me it was comfort food. When I sat at my grandparents' dining room table and took my first large bite of a gelatinous hoof, it was as if it had been seasoned with memory and marinated in love.

"So how's work?" Mama Win's eyes danced and pride dripped from her voice as she asked the question. I had not fallen into any of the traps that lay outside their front door. I had survived my first twenty-four years, when so many black men's lives were snuffed out. And a kind of communal gratitude surrounded me, as it did every time I went home.

"It's going fine, I'm working hard," I replied between bites.

"Now tell me again, what is it exactly that you do?" my grandfather asked.

This made me pause my energetic chewing for a moment. I wasn't sure what to tell him. I was a banker. But that's not really what he was asking. He knew I worked at a bank. His question was less about the title and more about, well, the work. In some ways, he was asking me the question that I had been avoiding asking myself.

I thought quickly. I was proud of the fact that, as I'd been taught and had repeated over and over again in the halls of the bank, we added liquidity to the markets. Liquidity ensured that businesses and governments had the capital they required to serve the needs of their clients and constituents. This was not shameful work; it was essential, at least in the system as it currently exists. I knew my lines, but I didn't know how to share them with my grandparents. They had lived in the same home for almost half a century. My grandfather led congregations and my grandmother led classrooms. Their pride was in the honesty and necessity of their labor—not just in the particularly complex economic system of the twenty-first century, but in a deeper, timeless way. People need faith; they need education. They always will. And that's what my grandparents did—they worked for other people in the most profound sense. That was what gave them their sense of pride. They were proud of me, too—their pride was constant and powerful, even though they had no idea what I did. They were just proud that I was doing something. That I was trying.

Before I could answer my grandfather's question, I was saved by my grandmother. She smiled at my grandfather and said, "Dear, you know he works at a bank. In fact, I am going to tell Mrs. Johnson she should go do her deposits with you." Mrs. Johnson was a neighbor who'd lived down the street from my grandparents for thirty-five years. My grandmother thought that I was a bank teller. That I could enter deposits on the first and fifteenth of the month and get people the cash from their paychecks. She had no idea that I wouldn't know what to do with Mrs. Johnson's deposit slip. And she had no idea that Mrs. Johnson probably couldn't get in to give it to me anyway, because she couldn't get past security in the building where I worked.

"Thanks, Mama Win, I would love that," was my only response. Then we all smiled and, mercifully, the subject was changed.

While I was occasionally roiled by deeper existential questions, my confidence in the level of work I was doing and in my ability to contribute increased every day. Assignments that used to take me the better part of a morning were now taking me fifteen minutes. Terms that would have meant absolutely zero to me just a year and a half before—exotic derivatives, compounding interest, exchange-traded funds, econometrics, options and futures—now had significance, resonance. I was living in London, hanging out with new friends, and better understanding not just banker lingo but the banker's lifestyle. I had opportunities, and I was using them the best I could. But taking opportunities clearly wasn't enough. I needed something more.

I watched the news with a soldier's eye. I was racing in place on a treadmill in a posh gym when the BBC broke the news that Saddam Hussein had been captured in a spider hole in Tikrit. My old friends, people I'd trained with in the military, were now preparing for their second deployment overseas. I publicly pledged my allegiance to my work and my colleagues—a ritual act of fidelity that business demands—while sneaking around to find out what was going on in the world beyond my spreadsheets. Keeping a window with obscure foreign policy websites open on my desktop computer, I felt like a teenage boy hiding his *Playboy* inside an algebra textbook. And then, suddenly, I was confronted with a stark choice that forced me to clarify where my heart was.

At the office, we had just ordered dinner to be delivered, a tradition that highlighted the rarity of dinner at home with family. My cell phone rang, and on the other end of the phone was Mike Fenzel, the former linebacker and combat officer who had drafted me for my summer with Homeland Security. I hadn't spoken to him in a while, so I quickly left the trading floor and darted into a stairwell to have some privacy.

"You enjoying being one of those masters of the universe?" Mike asked.

"It's fine. I'm really learning a lot. People here work really hard," I said.

"I'm sure they do," Mike replied. I could hear the smirk in his voice.

We quickly caught up, and then he moved on to the real point of the call.

"Wes, we have some fights going on. Are you ever going to jump in and help?"

My skin burned when he said it. He wasn't making an accusation, just stating a fact and asking a question, but his voice felt like my own conscience talking. Mike was one of my friends who already had multiple deployments under his belt. At this point, I had been an army officer for six years, and during three of those years we had been a nation at war. I had shed my own blood, sweat, and tears in training, but never in a situation where everything was on the line. It was all just training. That wasn't what Mike was talking about.

Mike had just been named deputy brigade commander of the 82nd Airborne Division, one of the most decorated and illustrious units in the United States military. He wasn't calling me to brag. He was calling to tell me it was time for me to help. I listened to his pitch, which sounded like this: *Forget the creature comforts you've become accustomed to, and forget about seeing your girlfriend or family for a year. But on the plus side, you get to go to the bathroom in burn pits, shower with baby wipes, and eat the best MREs the American taxpayer's dollar can buy.*

I sat on the white marble stairs on the sixteenth floor of Deutsche Bank's art-laden London headquarters, my right hand clutching my cell phone to my right ear, and my left hand playing with my navy blue tie as I heard him make the final part of his pitch: *You will see combat and be surrounded by people who want nothing more than to kill you and your soldiers. It will be tough, uncomfortable, and dangerous.*

Man, Mike sure knew how to make a pitch.

Mike and the 1st Brigade were leaving for Afghanistan in eight months. I had far less time than that to make a decision about whether I'd be leaving with them. We got off the phone with no commitment made, simply a promise on my part to think about it.

Seven years after making a pledge to the military (when I'd had to get my mother to sign the paperwork because I was not legally old enough to join the military on my own), I was now working in

London as a banker analyzing credit swaps. I debated with myself for days. I knew what my heart was telling me, but a pesky thing called "rational self-preservation" kept getting in the way. What Mike had called about was not military school. It was combat. An old and wise saying came to me: "The only people who glorify combat are those who have never seen it." And I knew from the stories of others that leading soldiers in combat can be an especially burdensome experience—you find that you would rather have something happen to you than the soldiers under your command. I had a flat in downtown London, a corporate credit card, a closet full of new clothes from designers I'd been told were really good. I had a job that many people, especially in those days before the financial crises to come, respected, even if they didn't quite understand it. Things were good and I was lucky.

So lucky that I wanted out.

■ ■ ■ ■ ■ ■ ■ ■ ■ ■ ■ ■ ■ ■ ■ ■ ■ ■ ■

The Believer

JOE MANKO

Principal, Liberty Elementary School

Sometimes we find that thing we're doing with our lives—which might be lucrative, or the end point of a lifelong dream—is not, in fact, the thing we do best. Shifting our focus, maybe even quitting, can be difficult, but often we find our work on a different path than the one we imagined. This was the lesson that transformed Joe Manko's life.

Joe Manko is an East Coast urban education warrior bred in the cushy sun-soaked suburbs of Huntington Beach, California. This freshly minted elementary school principal's soft-spoken demeanor belies his steely determination to take on Baltimore's notorious educational bureaucracy. His commitment is to give his impoverished students a level playing field and the tools to achieve what they can and want. Tall, slightly stooped, and bookish, the thirty-four-year-old Manko hardly looks the part of a gladiator for social justice. But he is.

"The desire to fight for kids is something that's been a slow build since I became a teacher in Baltimore ten years ago," he says. "There's so much injustice. Sometimes I feel that people in power take advantage of kids and communities because they don't feel they have the agency to say anything."

J oe Manko was born into a military family—his father, Edward Manko, is a retired Air Force lieutenant colonel turned financial adviser, and his mother, Kim, is a onetime Army nurse who became a social worker. Like countless other military brats, he's moved around a lot: before he was in third grade he'd moved from Texas to Hawaii, back to Texas, to Florida, then to San Pedro, California, before finally settling in Huntington Beach. Frequent uprooting tempered his spine, making him flexible and nimble, undaunted by challenge and change.

His mother, a Vietnamese immigrant, was a witness to the worst of the Vietnam War. Kim shared with her kids the horrors of war, its inherent unforgiving nature, and its zero-sum realities. Her knack for languages and her on-the-ground savvy got her an interpreter's job with the U.S. Navy. She worked her way up through the ranks and became the translator for one of the joint chiefs in charge of the Southeast Asian Theater. Ironically, it was her talent for language that allowed her to serve as both interpreter and counselor to the individuals who were leading the military campaigns that so scarred her.

Joe recounts his mother's tale: "One day she went into her boss's office and he asked her, 'If I could give you anything in the world, what would that be?' Without hesitating she said, 'I wish I could go to America and be able to take care of my family.' She saw coming to the U.S. as a way to make money to send back home." Though she spent several decades without her family, she eventually managed to sponsor uncles, cousins, and other family members to come to the United States as well. Once in America she went to school, joined the Army, became a nurse stationed in Hawaii, and met her future husband.

Meantime, Joe's father has his own backstory of resolute willpower. "My dad grew up in Michigan. His mother died when he was very young, maybe thirteen or fourteen. His dad was there but kind of absentee. Really, my father raised himself and my aunt."

Joe went through school knowing he wanted to make an impact, but he had no idea what that actually meant. He discovered his life's mission at Manual Arts High School in South Central Los Angeles, where once a week he'd teach a lesson on college and the value of persevering. "It was a totally different world. I'd never been anyplace like that. At that point I felt I'd been really sheltered in my first couple of years at UCLA, and I grew up in a pretty affluent suburb. I'd never seen poverty to this extent and the effects of it. I discovered I had a passion for working with kids from different socioeconomic strata. I was also coming to a better understanding of the concepts of wealth and privilege and realizing that education was an important vehicle for promoting social equity."

By the time he graduated from UCLA with a double major in history and political science and an education minor, his girlfriend, Frances, was already working with Teach for America (TFA) in Baltimore. TFA, launched by revolutionary leader Wendy Kopp, is a program that gives recent college graduates a chance to use their newly minted degrees to teach in some of the toughest urban and rural communities in our country. In 2011, 18 percent of Ivy League graduates applied to TFA. The program is not without its flaws or critics, but its impact on the educational landscape is undeniable, not just for students but for the teachers in the program, too.

"I got here following a girl," Joe now says, a blush glazing his ears. He speaks respectfully of Frances, who lured him to TFA and Baltimore only to dump him. "My first year here was tough emotionally. Frances and I broke up. And I was assigned to Booker T. Washington Middle School."

Joe wanted to work in urban education, and Booker T. was about as urban as Baltimore gets. The surrounding community had been ravaged by the crack epidemic of the 1980s and '90s and pestilential poverty. There were kids screaming at teachers, running down the halls, and throwing books out the window.

"When I got into the classroom, that was the first time I really, really struggled with anything. It was so hard. All around me TFA had these people who were very successful in everything they do, and then they got into the classroom and they were just miserable failures. I had an absolute inability to discipline."

There were fights and the occasional discovery that a student had brought a weapon to school, Joe says—the dramatic stuff that gets media attention. All this really pushed his belief that being an educator was for him. People told him, in some cases quite convincingly, that he had fulfilled his commitment. He had done the right thing by going to see how difficult "those kids" had it, and he could walk away feeling like he'd accomplished something. Joe had offers to join the corporate world; he had a chance to take the experience of teaching in a tough urban environment and use it to leverage entry into another, cushier environment. But Joe knew it was not that easy. "I could have left then and gone into a different, more lucrative world. But had I done that, could I honestly argue that the kids benefited at all? This work promised to be hard but fulfilling. I had seen the hard; now it was my job to work to make it fulfilling."

Despite the rough introduction to the city and teaching, by the end of his third year at Booker T., Joe was hooked. Instead of abandoning Baltimore and its underserved underclass, he signed on to teach at Rosemont Elementary and Middle School, two miles away. Rosemont was one of Baltimore's higher-performing schools, and Joe found it mind-shattering after Booker T. "The difference was hard to believe," he says, shaking his head. The two schools had similar demographics yet were worlds apart, one perpetually failing, the other successful.

He calls his first year at Rosemont, teaching sixth-grade language arts, his make-or-break year. "I could see why it would be hard to be successful in the classroom in a non-successful school, but in a successful school? That's what I had to face.

"I don't feel like I was ever a good teacher," he confesses. "I had a really hard time with managing student behaviors. I planned hard and thoroughly, but when it came to execution, I couldn't get students to listen to me. I had a steep learning curve when it came to instruction, but very gradual when it came to the kids."

Rosemont turned out to be a game-changer. Between 2005 and 2009, his teaching improved, but his most important discovery was unlocking the mystery of what set Rosemont apart from Booker T.: what he describes as "culture, climate, and leadership."

"There was more support for students and teachers at Rosemont. But the main thing was the principal, Sandy Ashe, and she was fantastic. She was a tiny woman but very powerful, a great leader and very loving. I remember at the very end of my interview, I reached out to shake her hand. She said, 'We don't do that here; we do hugs.'" Joe mimes how Ashe reached up and wrapped him tight. His face lights up at the memory.

With Ashe at the helm, Joe's intellect, drive, and empathy converged to make him a candidate, albeit a reluctant one, for a principalship. After spending time studying teaching in Japan and going through an innovative training program for principals called New Leaders for New Schools, he felt ready to take a position at one of Baltimore's institutions of learning. When the next school year started, he met his New Leaders mentor, Sonya Goodwyn-Askew, then principal at one of Baltimore's gems, Hilton Elementary School. "She was amazing," he says.

He credits her with igniting his "never take no for an answer" spirit. She showed Joe how to batter down the walls of bureaucratic resistance, navigate countless labyrinthine protocols, and understand the mountains of data. He took right to it.

"She taught me that you've just got to find the workaround. One of the things that's so problematic in urban schools is that people feel like they're running their heads into the wall over and over. They lose steam. She told me, 'If you're not getting the answer you want, you have to stay with it until you do. These are kids you're fighting for.' When people say you can't, that's not an answer. Nothing matters until the thing you need to get done gets done. People are going to try to wriggle out of things. People will throw up their hands and say, 'There's nothing I can do.' People try to create the idea that there's a terminus. Sonya taught me that can't be okay, because it's about the kids. You've got to harangue people. So I do."

Liberty Elementary, his current school, is his vision realized. Joe acknowledges that when he took over the school he fell into a "gold mine," with a strong community and "really, really good teachers with a tremendous work ethic and love for the kids." But the challenges his kids face are real and undeniable: 93 percent are living below the poverty line, and over 60 percent are growing up in single-parent households. Joe acknowledges the hardships Liberty confronts. They're typical of underresourced schools in underserved cities across the country. His response isn't to blame the families, the situation, or the environment. It's to take what many might figure to be his kids' greatest liabilities and turn those on their head, making grit, determination, and ingenuity their greatest strengths.

In his two short years, "Principal Joe" has slashed all middle management—he's the only administrator at Liberty—and poured the money typically earmarked for administrative costs (an assistant principal, for example) into classrooms and student support. That includes three part-time reading specialists and a handful of retired teachers who provide experienced instruction to small groups for an hour a day. He has introduced an innovative school-wide reading-based curriculum that allows teachers to accurately pinpoint each student's reading level and provide individualized support. With an infusion of enrollment-related budget money, Joe bought close to thirteen thousand books at various levels, from those aimed at fledgling readers to those for the most advanced, and created a library of book bins in each classroom. All the students know their starting level and can track their progress as they move through the bins, which are labeled by level. He led the charge on a program to introduce iPads, the first of its kind in the Baltimore school system. With 120 devices in the school, the program allows kids in some kindergarten, first-grade, third-grade, and fifth-grade classes to take ownership of an iPad in school for the entire academic year; second and fourth graders have laptops. These become each kid's portal to learning. Kids in the third through fifth grades who are not in the classes using iPads get exposure to technology in either their reading and social studies or math and science classes. "It's innovative by Baltimore standards, and it's issues of class that makes it innovative for us. In Arlington, Virginia, every kid already has one. We've trying to give our kids the same advantage."

Joe has never forgotten the lesson that Sandy Ashe taught him when she got up and hugged him instead of shaking hands when they first met. The feeling of that embrace never left him, and now he shares that feeling every day with every one of his students. When his students come in every morning, he greets them with not simply a smile but a hug and an "I love you." From the moment they walk through the door they know they are not only in a place of high expectations but also in a place of peace and freedom—a place of love.

Joe walks with easy comfort in the community he's made his turf. He wishes a few people good afternoon, and waves at a volunteer fixing up the school grounds. As he shows a visitor the school, he explains how the open classrooms actually enhance learning, even though they might seem like a recipe for chaos: "More adults watching the kids. Older kids setting examples for the younger ones. It's hard to grasp, but it works so well. Our kids really want to learn." Modesty competes with pride in his voice and on his face.

His words come fast, but they're well chosen. He's working on his latest project: the crafty confiscation and reopening of a freshly imagined community center adjacent to his school. He points out the field where kids will get to ride horses, a deal he put together as part of the reimagined center. The center, which will have neighborhood-centric, learning-driven programming for all age groups designed to foment ground-up social change, is Joe's object of obsession as he wrestles unfinished agreements and equipment and cash shortages into submission. He discusses the possibilities of early childhood education and career development with mounting zeal. His hands draw his vision in the air with small descriptive gestures, and his soft dark eyes under expressive thick black brows become laser beams tracking the future of his students and the generations to come.

And it will happen one hug at a time.

3

■ ■ ■ ■ ■ ■ ■ ■ ■ ■

The Lesson of the Soldier

Finding Your Fight

After I made the decision to join the 82nd Airborne's mission in Afghanistan, my biggest concern was telling my girlfriend, Dawn. I hoped and prayed that this would not ruin my chances with the woman with whom I hoped to spend the rest of my life.

I'd heard about Dawn Flythe long before I met her, and the word was all good: I heard she was beautiful and smart, a politically savvy firecracker who was as dedicated to public service as I hoped to be. When I called her up to ask her for a date, she was working on a get-out-the-vote campaign. As we got closer, she accompanied me everywhere from London to South Africa.

I knew Dawn was an incredible woman, and I wanted her to be my wife. She knew that I was a captain in the army, but being in the reserves can deceive even the people closest to you about the nature of your commitment. My day-to-day life wasn't the life of a man in uniform. Yet she understood and supported my decision to go to Afghanistan. Moreover, she understood that there were no safe theaters in a war. While most people at this point were focused on the much hotter war in Iraq and said, "Thank God you're going to Afghanistan," Dawn knew better. "Just come home safe," she told me. And like so many thousands of soldiers before me, I promised her that I would, and then I prayed that this was a promise I wouldn't break.

I called Mike a few days after our initial conversation and told him I wanted to join him and the 82nd Airborne down in Fort Bragg and deploy with them wherever they were going. Mike was thrilled. So was I. I was ready for this new adventure, and to fulfill a promise I had made to myself a long time ago. I was a soldier, and I was trained to lead troops. The military—for all of the horrors inherent in its mission—had saved my life. My friends were fighting for their lives now. I owed them. And I was excited to fulfill my obligation.

My next conversations were not nearly as easy. Though Dawn knew, I had to inform everyone else of this sudden change: the people I worked with, my friends, my grandparents, and my mom.

For some people, I knew, the best way to couch it was to describe it as a "call-up," where I had no choice but to say yes. "I guess it's just my time," is how I would begin the conversation, noting my good luck that while many soldiers had already been deployed on multiple occasions, this would be my first time heading overseas with an M-4 rifle instead of a passport and a camera. But the hardest conversations of all were the ones with my family.

No matter how I broke it, everyone who heard the news looked stunned. They knew in some abstract way that I was an army officer, but they'd never connected the young banker in the suit with the two wars now raging in the Middle East and Asia. Hugging commenced, tears flowed, prayers began.

It was in those moments that I began to understand that deployments can be roughest on the ones left behind. While deployed, soldiers have good days and bad days, successes and failures. But we experience all of them together: we are there for one another to celebrate, commiserate, bitch and moan, boast, embrace, mourn. These friends understand what we're feeling without needing us to provide a whole lot of explanation. Many families back home don't have that. Mostly what the ones left behind have is the daily, often isolated suffering of wondering if their loved ones are in mortal danger.

People didn't say much when I told them I'd be leaving, but I got a lot of looks. There was the look of concern and pity, as if I'd just told them I had a week left to live. Or the look of heartbreak, like they wanted to offer me some positive words but couldn't think of anything to say.

The one point that nearly everyone made was how lucky I was to be headed to Afghanistan. Back in 2005, when I made the decision to deploy, all of the news was about Iraq: the thousands of coalition casualties (most of them U.S. soldiers), the flawed elections mired in violence, the suicide bomb attacks that killed so many Iraqis, the "stop-loss" policy that kept thousands of U.S. troops in Iraq well past the point at which they'd expected to be rotated home, the Abu Ghraib prisoner abuse scandal. Again and again, I heard, "Thank God you are going to Afghanistan."

What most of them didn't know, because it was below the radar of the Iraq-focused media, was that during the same period, Afghanistan was seeing heavy fighting. The U.S. military was being asked to patrol a hostile nation that had a landmass larger than Texas, but to do it with fewer than seventeen thousand troops.

After managing to evade U.S. forces and Northern Alliance troops three years earlier, the remnants of the Taliban had gradually begun to regain their confidence and recruit both Pashtun loyalists and international jihadis to wage a renewed offensive against coalition forces and the Afghan government. And the area we were about to be deployed to, Khost, sat right on the border of Afghanistan and Pakistan, in the heart of the fight.

"Yep," I'd agree, ignoring the fluttering in my stomach. "Thank God I'm just heading to Afghanistan."

Our training in preparation for deployment was intense. There were physical endurance tests to prepare us for combat in the desolate mountainous regions of Afghanistan; regular drills to help us distinguish between a stack of trash on the side of a road and a deadly improvised explosive device (IED) waiting to detonate; tests on cleaning, assembling, and loading your weapon in complete darkness. We took language lessons in both Pashtu and Urdu, two of the more than forty languages spoken in Afghanistan (with an additional two hundred dialects). This mosaic of linguistic complexity merely underlined the untidiness resulting from the country's founding and history. None of us were expected to become fluent Pashtu-speakers, but some of the first words we were taught mapped out the intricately layered work we were embarking on:

Manana	Thanks
Sa khidmath shta?	Is there anything I can do?
Bakhana ghwarum	I ask for your forgiveness
Wasla dee parmzaka kegda	Put down your weapon

We had combat veterans both as instructors and as guest speakers, which helped add an important sense of context to our training. Every time it started to seem like our classroom lectures and simulated drills were redundant or absurd, a recent vet would come in and share his or her story. The stories were always different, but they all had a frighteningly similar message: *You can die out there. Lack of preparation or focus will get you and your soldiers killed.*

"War sucks, gentlemen," our company's commander, Captain Glover, told us. He'd just completed two deployments, one to Afghanistan and one to Iraq. "Anyone who celebrates it or is quick to enter into it has either never seen it up close or does not have direct contact with anyone who has to fight in it."

I read everything I could about Afghanistan before deploying: its history, its culture, its terrain. Steve Coll's *Ghost Wars* showed how the rise of the Taliban and the sanctuary that created for Al-Qaeda were directly attributable to international neglect, indifference, and naiveté. *Inside the Soviet Army in Afghanistan*, by Alexander Alexiev, did a brilliant job of showing how military might and infrastructure has never, and will never, be enough to change a country or, more important, a culture. Neither book was particularly encouraging about American prospects in Afghanistan, but it was important for me to understand the political context of the war; I didn't want to kill or die without knowing why. And as someone who would be leading other soldiers, I wanted to do everything I could to maximize our chances for success. To me that included making an honest appraisal of those chances, and even figuring out the origins of the conflict we were now involved in.

I also read novels. Fiction such as *Hindu Kush* and *The Kite Run-*

ner never allowed me to forget the humanity of the people whose country we were invading. It is far too easy to stereotype and caricature those you're in conflict with, which only makes you cynical, hateful, or overconfident—or all three. It also coarsens you. I thought a lot about how many American soldiers were inspired to fight this battle by the heroic humanism of those first responders on 9/11, the ones who sacrificed their lives for strangers of all backgrounds in those burning towers. It would be a great tragedy, I thought, if we'd come to this part of the world with such high ideals only to dehumanize a whole population, just for the sake of our own survival. But I also didn't want to be naive. This was war, as Captain Glover reminded us. It was supposed to be challenging and noble and done with great commitment. And yes, it was supposed to suck.

No amount of reading or personal testimony could have prepared me for what I encountered when we left the safe confines of the Tillman USO Center, our first stop, and arrived at Forward Operating Base (FOB) Salerno in Khost, the location that would be our home for the next year. The Tillman Center—named after Pat Tillman, the football player turned Army Ranger—is one of the largest bases in the country, complete with a Burger King, a secure infrastructure, and creature comforts you wouldn't expect to see in a combat zone. FOB Salerno was located in eastern Afghanistan, snuggled against the mountainous border region between Afghanistan and Pakistan and the infamous Federally Administered Tribal Areas (FATA). Khost had been the base of operations for the Soviets during their ill-fated occupation of Afghanistan during the 1980s; it was also where Pat Tillman had lost his life. Now it would become the staging area for our collection of paratroopers.

•   •   •

As our choppers hovered just above the ground, preparing for our landing in Khost, clouds of dust and dirt engulfed us through the open chopper doors. When we landed we grabbed our heavy-duty military duffle bags, which contained everything we would need for a year. Looking ahead, we saw a few hard-shell infrastructures but mainly a collection of stand-alone green tents. These would be our accommodations.

Within hours of arriving, we had our first security briefing. Each base in Afghanistan was different, with different rules. How we did it at FOB Salerno was going to be totally different from how it was done at Gardez or Jalalabad or Bagram. Because of its strategically important location, Khost was home to some of the most dangerous fighting in Afghanistan. I frantically scribbled notes as we were told to make sure to put all our paperwork in brown paper trash bags at the end of every day, so they could be burned. All mail we received from back home should be removed from the envelopes to ensure that the addresses of our loved ones never got into the wrong hands. We were to have our weapons on us at all times, no exceptions. There was "100 percent light discipline" in the evenings, meaning that only red and green lights were to be used after dark—those colors were tougher to detect from long distances, and also wouldn't affect night vision goggles as much. Every time we "left the wire"—that is, went beyond the walls of the FOB—we had to be in full gear, and even if your mission was scheduled to be only a few hours, you packed at least a full day's worth of equipment, gas, and food.

At the conclusion of the briefing we all got to our feet and stood at attention while the commander strode confidently from the room. We had work to do, and it was to begin immediately. I looked at my watch. Only months before, at this time of day I'd still be behind my desk in London, or perhaps at a pub running up a nice tab. Now I was standing on the dirt floor of a tent in Khost with a notebook full of reminders that—just as Mike had promised—I was surrounded by people who wanted to kill me. The words of my family and friends echoed through the back of my mind: *Thank God you are going to Afghanistan.*

My job was to lead a team of paratroopers who were trained in civil affairs, psychological operations, information operations, and a collection of other special operations command disciplines. Our broad, enigmatic job description was to collect and protect information, work with allies on the Afghan side, and aggressively pursue enemies of the Afghan people. But this wasn't a job in any traditional sense of the word. There were no set hours or consistent routine—only constant, harrowing uncertainty.

Our work was primarily with the Afghan people, of course. I quickly realized who the enemy was—and it was not them. Soldiers—including me at times, I'm embarrassed to say—used nicknames for the Afghan people that, even when they were in and of themselves inoffensive, were designed to dehumanize them: "haji," "boy lovers." These were similar to the names that were given to Iraqis, and to the Vietnamese, Japanese, and Germans before them. They were similar to the names given to immigrants and black people within our own country—the kinds of names used for my own grandparents when they traveled the American South or when they tried to get a mortgage in the American North. But we weren't there to fight a people or culture or a religion. Our enemy was an ideology embodied by the warlords, terrorists, and insurgents who made it impossible to establish stable peace and governance in the country. Our job was to fight these bad actors. But our job was not to defeat the Afghan people—that would be insane. *We were in their country.*

Abdullah was a local Afghan who began working with my team as a "terp," or interpreter. He was in his early twenties, a lanky five feet eight inches tall; his mustache and voluminous beard covered much of his handsome face but could not hide his broad smile. That smile was especially noteworthy when you consider the life Abdullah had lived before I had the pleasure of meeting him.

Abdullah was born to a former soldier, a junior officer in the Afghan army—the same army that was proudly celebrated after driving the powerful Soviet military back over the border. By the late 1980s, the Soviet Union had begun to understand that victory in Afghanistan could not be achieved. More than thirty thousand Soviet soldiers had died, and well over a million Afghans had lost their lives. Mikhail Gorbachev, then general secretary of the Communist Party of the Soviet Union, began to rapidly withdraw forces from the landlocked nation. On the surface it looked as though the American strategy of supporting the Afghans in their struggle against the Soviets had worked: the drawn-out hostilities had helped to financially deplete the war-weary Soviets without a drop of American blood being spilled. But Afghanistan was now a country destroyed by war, devastated by the death of a generation of young men, and riddled with power vacuums waiting to be filled by those with the biggest guns. And guns were everywhere.

Like many Afghan soldiers, after the war Abdullah's father returned to his hometown, the eastern Afghanistan city of Asadabad, to reunite with his family. But he found that with the Soviets gone, the Afghans had now been forgotten by the international community, the same community that had freely supplied them with arms to fight the Soviet Union. Afghanistan was left without any trading partners or the basic infrastructure needed for robust internal trade. It was simply an opium-rich nation with a plethora of weapons. The country fell into years of civil war between rival forces, warlords, and religious fundamentalists. As the Taliban emerged as the dominant force in the country, a form of sharia law was eventually imposed over much of the land, dictating, among other things, a drastically reduced place for women in Afghan life. Women were no longer allowed to be educated past the age of eight, and even then they were allowed to learn only the Koran. In one well-documented incident, when a group of Taliban soldiers discovered a woman running an informal school in her apartment, the students were beaten and the woman was thrown down a flight of stairs, breaking her leg, before she was imprisoned. Women who were found guilty of "crimes" such as flirting would have acid thrown in their faces. And the Taliban's laws went beyond just the degradation of women. For both men and women there were public beheadings in stadiums, and the hands of those found guilty of theft were cut off. The Taliban's bastardized form of Islam became law in any land they occupied.

The Taliban eventually achieved a partial triumph in the civil wars, occupying the Afghan capital, Kabul, and officially imposing their brutal form of sharia over the majority of the country. Many Afghan men, including Afghan veterans such as Abdullah's father, were not happy. They'd fought for Afghan independence against foreign invasion, and Abdullah's father questioned whether strict Afghan laws like these—which some people associated with fundamentalists from the Arab world rather than home-grown Afghani Islamic practice—were markedly better than foreign involvement. He voiced his concerns and let his opinions be known. The Taliban figured if Abdullah's father couldn't control his tongue, they would render him voiceless. When Abdullah was only nine years old his father's throat was slit by the Taliban, who left the dead body in front of his house for his family to find. Abdullah's mother vanished at the same time, leaving Abdullah and his siblings alone in the world.

Eventually Abdullah and two of his siblings found their way to a refugee camp in southern Afghanistan, and with the help of an international aid organization he was able to spend five years going to school in the United Kingdom, during which time he was separated from—and lost contact with—his siblings and other family members. He returned home to Afghanistan as a young teenager, at an age when his peers were entering manhood. In many ways he'd crossed that threshold long before. Upon his return, he saw that the stranglehold of the Taliban had only tightened—and it would continue to tighten leading up to his twenty-first birthday, when the attacks of 9/11 once again changed everything in his country.

Like his father before him, Abdullah wanted to be part of a new, less oppressive Afghanistan. He decided to support the coalition forces' efforts to uproot the Taliban and help establish a new Afghan government to rebuild the country. He was not a warrior like his father, he realized—he would not join the Afghan National Army, nor the Afghan National Police or the Afghan Special Forces, groups we also worked closely with. He was uncomfortable around blood. Loud noises make him jump, almost comically. But we needed Pashtu- and English-speaking terps, and Abdullah quickly signed up to join the effort. A year after he began working with the U.S. Army, he was assigned to me.

Terps were paid well relative to the average Afghan worker,

whose annual income was under $500, but the job was not without its risks. Not only did Abdullah go on missions with us, which were laden with immediate dangers, but the remaining Taliban and insurgent forces made it clear that anybody who worked with the coalition forces was not safe. Abdullah would tell me about "night letters" that many terps and others who supported the coalition forces received. He would get up in the morning and find a letter left at his door; it was always a variation on "We know you are working against the Afghan people, and if you continue you and your entire family will be killed."

Knowing this, I sometimes asked Abdullah why he continued working as a terp. Usually he would just smile and shrug. But once he told me he was tired of the fear the Taliban spread and relied on for their control. He was tired of his people being frightened of them. "They are strong, but I am not scared," he said. "I look forward to the day when our country will not have to worry about them anymore."

As was the case with a lot of Afghans, Abdullah's primary loyalty was not necessarily to the nation he called home. Afghanistan had emerged as an independent nation in 1741, but the "national" concept of Afghanistan remained a shaky one. In Afghanistan, a person's loyalty was first and foremost with the immediate family and then the extended clan. After family, loyalty spread to one's tribe. Abdullah fought as much for the legacy of his family as anything else. I remember on one patrol we were handing out supplies to a group of Afghans, and among the items we were distributing were flags that carried a beautiful silhouette of Afghanistan filled in with black, red, and green, Afghanistan's national colors. One villager started speaking to Abdullah in Pashtu, with a clouded expression on his face. After their conversation ended, I asked

Abdullah what was the conversation about. Abdullah explained to me the man had not understood the significance of the image on the flag, so Abdullah told him it was a picture of Afghanistan—a picture of his country. At that, the man had shrugged and walked away. That's when I started to understand that our goal of establishing loyalty to a national government was possibly in trouble.

Abdullah, on the other hand, wondered about my loyalty to the U.S. armed forces. He told me that many times when we went on patrols, Afghan people and particularly children would come up to him and ask him what country I was fighting for. They were very used to foreign soldiers in their country—after all, this was a nation that had been in a constant state of war for the past thirty years and had seen sporadic conflict for centuries before that—but they were not used to seeing someone like me. Since Abdullah had spent time in the United Kingdom he understood that not every Westerner was blond-haired and blue-eyed, as the movies often portrayed, so the fact that I was black was not so strange to him. But he'd also learned quite a bit about the struggle that black Americans have had in United States, from slavery to Jim Crow, to voter ID laws and educational and criminal justice disparities. It was not clear to him that black people in America were not themselves a conquered and systematically oppressed population.

I explained to him about the extraordinary progress my country had made in race relations, and how it was my ancestors—and the ancestors of other Americans of all colors and creeds—who often pushed the country to be greater, broader, more democratic, and freer. I gave him my full American pitch: about how America was a large experiment, and with every generation we struggle to expand and live up to our greatest ideals, to be greater in the future than we were in the past. I told him I fought for my country because I love it, flaws and all. I fought for it because the people who make up our beautiful, diverse tapestry deserve to be fought for. I fought for it so that this experiment can continue, so that we have a chance to become the country that my grandparents dreamed of and that my grandchildren deserve.

"It seems as though we fight for the same things, then," Abdullah replied.

The last time I saw Abdullah was a few days before we were scheduled to head home. I introduced him to the "new me," the member of the 101st Airborne Division who would be taking over my responsibilities. Then I pulled Abdullah in for a hug.

"Until we meet again, my friend," I said

"Yes, Captain," he replied.

I have not seen Abdullah since, but I often think about him, his family, and his safety. I also worry. Years after my redeployment back to the States, I know his dream of a Taliban-less country could not be further from reality.

I fell in love with the Afghan people because what they wanted— or at least what a vast majority of them wanted—was what a vast majority of us want: a safe place to live, a way to provide food to their families and ensure their health, a chance for happiness. It takes different contours in different places and is articulated in different idioms, but at the core, our wants are starkly similar. So are our difficulties.

For instance, the tenets of Pashtunwali, essentially the ethical code of the Pashtun people, are not so different from the codes that exist in many American communities. At its core, Pashtunwali ultimately derives from demonstrations of loyalty and courage. Pashtunwali was what kept Marcus Luttrell alive in July 2005 when his entire SEAL team was killed beside him and a group of Afghan villagers helped him survive, as documented in his bestselling book. But there is another edge to that sword, and that is the ideal among Pashtuns that violations of honor must be avenged. All insults, regardless of how minor, must be addressed, often in blood. If the culprit flees before justice can be administered, the blood of his closest male relative must be shed. This was unfortunately not a foreign concept to many of us who had witnessed the bloodshed that takes place in so many American cities. In a June weekend in my hometown of Baltimore in 2013, for instance, twenty people were shot. After the smoke dissipated and the smell of gunpowder began to fade, eventually it was learned that the initial beef had started after two rival drug dealers from two different parts of town got into a fistfight in a local bar over one of the dealers disrespecting the girlfriend of the other. After the fight that night, two people were shot to death, the victor of the initial fistfight and one of his associates. What happened during the remainder of the weekend was a collection of retaliatory hits against civilians—essentially collateral damage. While Pashtunwali carried an Afghan name, the concepts underlying it were not exclusive to Afghanistan.

This is, of course, the deepest irony of this war and many other conflicts: our lives are most disrupted and put at risk by the actions of a small number of people who somehow want something different from what the majority of us want. I knew enough about the history of America to be aware that its darkest moments have always been driven by power-mad demagogues who manage to convince people that it's somehow in their best interests to oppress their fellow citizens or senselessly attack people on the other side of the world. I know that the oppression is compounded when the will of that vocal and merciless few is amplified by the silence of countless more. As Edmund Burke potently said, "All it takes for evil to triumph is for good people to do nothing."

I know enough about American communities to know that the violence of a few outlaws is enough to leave a whole neighborhood in fear. I've learned enough about the history of Afghanistan to know that the simple desires of regular Afghans had often fallen victim to the power games of a handful of leaders of the so-called great powers—and that the miserable rise of the Taliban, an extreme and disciplined minority who seized power in a moment of chaos, was in many ways an outgrowth of those distant and pointless struggles. Meanwhile, most of us—Afghan, American, whatever—just wanted a safe place to raise our families, a chance for happiness, an opportunity to pursue our passions and beliefs. But there we were: Abdullah, alone in the world and awakening to death threats, but still fighting for a better country; me, carrying my own weight in body armor and weapons a million miles from home, fighting to keep my country safe so that it can keep evolving toward its destiny. An amazingly unlikely union, one that at the time made beautiful sense.

I came to Afghanistan for a mix of reasons—duty, loyalty to an institution that had saved me and to the friends I'd trained with, and a sense that in the wake of 9/11 I had a part to play in making things right. Once I was there, I operated like any soldier, following the chain of command. But in a deeper sense, my mission in Afghanistan had very little to do with the policy machinations back in Washington—I was not risking my life every day because I believed so deeply in the specific policies articulated by the president or secretary of defense. I did, however, believe in the authority of the president of the United States to direct the military; and I believed in the deeper mission of the United States in the world as I saw it.

Even if the institutions we are part of are flawed, we can still find a way to fight if we believe in the larger mission. My conversations with Abdullah taught me that. Did Abdullah believe in a united Afghanistan? I'm not sure. Did he believe in the United States, the country he was helping—and putting his life at risk to help? Not particularly. But he was loyal to the country he found in his family, in the memories of the loved ones he'd lost, and in the people he knew. And he fought not for some large geopolitical rationale but for the simplest reason: he wanted them to be free to pursue their own happiness, free of the oppressions of the Taliban. Working with the United States was his way of doing it. The irony revealed by our conversations was that I wasn't so different from him.

In addition to falling for the Afghan people I met, another love affair developed, and that was with my soldiers. I adored their passion and their hearts. I knew everything about them: Which ones were having financial or marital issues. Which ones were motivated by carrots, which were motivated by sticks. Which ones were planning on making the military a career and which ones were planning on stepping out of uniform as soon as their deployments ended and never stepping back into one again. I made it my business to know them, to be open and available to them even when I myself was exhausted and weary, because that was essential to leading them effectively. In order for soldiers to follow you, they need to respect you. Soldiers will always acknowledge the chain of command, but the best leaders endear themselves to their soldiers beyond the obligations of rank. As my mother used to say about adolescents, "Kids need to think that you care before they care what you think." In many ways, soldiers are the same way. If they feel a sense of vested interest, there is nothing they won't do for a leader.

Despite the dire circumstances and our often grim surrounding, my time in Afghanistan energized me. For the first time in a long time, I felt like I mattered. We had good days and bad days, but at the end of each day, you could lay your head down and know that your being there meant something to the soldiers you worked with. That sense of purpose and relevance was something I'd been yearning for, I realized, all during the time I'd spent running spreadsheets in London, and I finally tasted it.

About three months into the deployment I had just come back from a mission with our team. I was placing my Kevlar helmet on a hook in the Secure Compartmented Information Facility (SCIF), a central place of communication for the brigade, when Sergeant Johnson walked up to me. His North Carolina stomp and 82nd Airborne swagger met you before he even opened his mouth. "Hey, sir, Colonel Fenzel needs to see you."

"Roger, thanks," I replied. I figured it was simply Mike wanting to check in with me to see how things were going. The deployment had been good thus far, but tough. Mike understood that NCOs and officers spend so much time focusing on their soldiers—their health and welfare, their physical challenges, their mental states— that in many cases they forget to think about themselves, so as I knocked on his door I assumed he was just going to ask me how I was doing.

"Sir, you wanted to see me?"

"Come in, Wes," he said, and got right to the point: "Wes, I want to talk to you about what you need to do after redeployment."

We were only three months in, and I had almost a full year to go before my deployment was up. To be terribly honest, none of us tried to think much about the end of our deployment or what we'd do after—thinking about anything other than the mission in front of you while you're in a combat zone could be costly. It was also considered bad luck.

Mike continued, "It's important that the folks making policy in Washington understand your experiences, your perspective after serving over here."

"You got it, sir." I told Mike I would do some research and get back to him.

As I posted out of his office, though, I was already thinking about the mission for tomorrow.

THE WORKER #3

■ ■ ■ ■ ■ ■ ■ ■ ■ ■ ■ ■ ■ ■ ■ ■ ■ ■

The Healers

JOHN GALINA AND DALE BEATTY
Founders, Purple Heart Homes

No one goes off to war and returns unchanged. This certainly applies to millions of veterans who come home and use the skills they acquired to earn a living and build a life at home. But it also applies to the soldiers who return with challenges—both visible and invisible.

So many of us have to deal with the aftermath of traumatic events that seem to create a sharp line of demarcation in our lives between who we were before and who we became after. There's no one way to make sense of trauma or "get over it." But one of the gifts of our returning veterans is the variety of ways they've worked at figuring out how you move ahead in life when you have been dramatically changed by an event—how the project of finding your work can go on. After having fought a war, they are still finding their fight—the larger fight of making their lives meaningful.

John Galina and Dale Beatty are a pair of thirty-four-year-old veterans of the Iraq War who have devoted themselves to building homes for returning veterans with special needs. They are a remarkable example of how finding the work of our lives can sometimes come from our darkest moments—moments when we can sometimes see with the greatest clarity.

"Happy Alive Day."

"To you too, brother."

John Galina and Dale Beatty are shooting off fireworks to celebrate their seventh Alive Day, a November 15 celebration of survival, creation, and defiance. Alive Day is a rebirth, a celebration of an event that didn't happen. It's when veterans reflect on the day they should have died but were spared—an incident that reshaped their life but didn't take it. The phenomenon did not originate with veterans of Iraq and Afghanistan; this is a tradition that has been going on in the veterans community since at least the Vietnam War and possibly earlier. But this new batch of war vets have taken on the mantle of celebration and reflection with particular vigor.

John and Dale have had their fates fused since 1996, when they were both seventeen-year-old students enlisted in the same National Guard reserve unit. Both men struggled with finding satisfying full-time work after high school. John became a full-time general contractor. Dale worked as a cook at Cracker Barrel before signing on with the National Guard full-time. When John got a call from Dale about joining him in active duty in September 2003,

he didn't hesitate: he reenlisted in the Army National Guard, joining a unit with Dale as his sergeant.

"We just have that relationship. We share the same core values,
the same history in our families of military service," says Dale, the
affection palpable. "I knew I could trust John in a foxhole. If I'm
driving down the road and he's in the vehicle behind me, we know
what we're willing to do for each other. It's something you just
feel—it's not something you talk about. That's what it's like over
there. You gotta be tight with everybody. If I'm not certain this
person is going to carry me off the battlefield, it's not someone I
want next to me."

Before they ever set a boot in Iraq, their stateside deployments
forged and tempered their two-halves-of-a-whole relationship.
When Hurricanes Floyd and Fran devastated portions of North
Carolina three years apart, the two teenagers, looking to see how
far they could push their limits, were in there "rescuing refugees
out of their houses, water about to come in their front door," recalls Dale, running a hand through his close-cropped hair. "And
we're walking through floodwaters getting people to safe, high, dry
ground . . . John and I weren't the guys sitting back eating or laying
on a cot for twelve hours. We'd take an extra shift to go help. The
fire chief is on for twenty-four hours and asks us for another mission, John and I look at each other and say, 'Yeah, let's go. Let's go
out there and make a difference.'"

John, vigilant, thoughtful, and well-spoken, acknowledges they
both thrived on adrenaline rush, the exultation of wading into impossible situations and making good things happen. "We pulled a
mentally challenged kid out of a house that was under eight feet of
water [during Hurricane Floyd]," he recalls. "He was floating on a
mattress."

But these domestic missions were startlingly different from the overseas combat missions they would soon experience.

They landed in Kuwait, and "it took us about two weeks to get used to the heat. We'd just come from winter on the East Coast. And yeah, it was winter there in Kuwait, too, but different. You can't go outside without sunglasses, and you need to drink two gallons of water a day to keep from passing out. You might be thinking it's not so bad and it's 140 degrees. Especially inside a vehicle, it can be that hot or hotter. I have a picture of the thermometer at midnight and it's 115 degrees."

When they arrived in Iraq, their welcome was brutal. Drills and downtime were rare, operation tempo was high. There was no training that could have prepared them for the 24/7 intensity of the operations. "We saw other units come back into the base, washing blood out of their trucks after a really bad mission. We'd drive down the road and see vehicles—a Humvee mangled and burned down to nothing. We destroyed the vehicle and wouldn't leave it for them. Our training was clear and certain. Trained to react to contact. Trained to react with overwhelming force."

They were also trained to look like a hard target: attentive and alert, developing a mean persona and an assertiveness that they used everywhere they went. They honed their ability to take in everything around them, looking for IEDs, insurgents, and snipers.

Despite everything they had to think about and focus on, one thing stayed at the forefront of their minds. "Every day I thought, 'All nine of my guys in my squad are going to come home alive,'" John remembers. "I would try to be more loyal to my squad than to leadership and the directives we got. We still got the mission accomplished, maybe just not the way the orders were given. There were all kinds of stressful encounters because of that. I was obviously doing the right thing. Bad commanders play by the book all the time; good commanders let their people make decisions. It was a hard fourteen months."

"We worked with local nationals a lot," Dale says. "That was poverty I've never seen. No floors, no windows, flies all over the kids' faces and they didn't even care. People have no idea. It's easy to become jaded with this society when people get upset because there's a nick on a $2 million wall. Fighting over there, I could see the logic of winning over the people. Only 2 percent of the population in Iraq were our enemies. The rest were scared or hated us because they'd been programmed to hate us. It's difficult when you see kids your own kids' age and they have nothing and there is nothing."

He wonders now about the families they'd see all the time that lived next to the base. The squad had taken on a mission to stop indirect fire onto the base. "We'd go out and hide in the middle of the night and wait for those people to come. We were there enough so that they thought shooting at us was a bad idea. We'd see the same Bedouins, farmers and shepherds. Maybe we'd give them a case of water. In the desert if you give someone a case of water, they're going to talk to you. We were gathering human intelligence and working with those people on a daily basis. You get to see what their world is, their daily lives, their children, and families. It stays with you."

The deployment was tough. They endured multiple attacks. Once insurgents drove a car packed with explosives into the gate of the base and killed twenty-three people, mostly Iraqis who worked on the base. Some were kids ten to twelve years old; some were older, fifty-, sixty-, or seventy-year-olds who'd come to work on the base for $1 a day. They were people in line waiting to be searched so that they could come and work various jobs: hauling rocks, picking up machine gun brass on the shooting range, delivering water.

"The carnage was unbelievable," John says. "We had two medics in our squad who saved a number of lives, including Iraqis injured. That bomb hit me pretty hard. A lot of kids were killed during that attack. Most people don't get it. You've got to clean that mess up. You can't leave those twenty dead bodies outside your front gate. We were on the base reactionary force. My squad was the one that responded to attacks. Our job was to go secure the area. We caught one of the suicide bombers who got stuck in the car and the other got away. One American soldier was hurt, but none severely. I don't know how anybody really dealt with it. You've got to find greater purpose in life and greater reason. You get over it by trying to do something good every day."

One overcast day in November, with John driving and Dale riding shotgun on a trip like any other, an undetected land mine blew their Humvee sky high. John says he was the only one not ejected from the Humvee. "They thought I was dead. I was left for forty-five minutes. Dale's got parts spread out over a hundred meters. Here we are in the middle of the desert, four in our vehicle injured, and he's got half of both feet missing.

"One of our squad leaders finally pulled me out of the vehicle. The vehicle was upside down and I was laying on the roof in a pool of blood. I was completely unconscious. I don't even remember being pulled out of the vehicle. I remember waking up in the desert, someone giving me water, and my eyes were matted shut. I thought I'd lost my eyesight."

Dale, on the other hand, remembers everything. "I knew what was happening, I had been to combat lifesaver training—a regular soldier who can give an IV. I'm no medic, but we were educated about shock, blood loss, and all that. I knew I needed IVs in me, and I knew I was going into shock."

Dale continued, "As soon as I woke I knew both legs were gone. I remember them treating me. My leg was at a 180-degree angle from where it was supposed to be. They brought the stretcher next to me and I rolled. My right leg was almost completely broken in half. The sole of the boot was in my face. That's the first thing I saw. I remember getting IVs, getting on the helicopter, and talking to the anesthesiologist in the field hospital."

He also remembers that John found him in the field hospital. "John snuck back in an area he wasn't supposed to be in because he wanted to come and find me and talk to me. He, in his bloody uniform, tracked me down and snuck back to where I was. Other people might not have taken that chance, but John Galina does."

From the moment Dale was hit, he got the best of care. During the year he spent recuperating at Walter Reed Hospital, he and his wife, Belinda, and their two kids stayed for free at Fisher House Foundation, a special housing unit for wounded vets and their families. "Having your family around when you're hurt is the best medicine. Finally the Department of Defense and the Veterans Administration recognize that having your family next to you is what makes you heal."

Dale knew he was fortunate. While in the hospital, he'd see a wife or girlfriend coming to visit a husband or boyfriend, take one look at a missing limb, and walk out or file for divorce. He had rock-solid support, and he was aware that this set him apart.

"With me being severely wounded, I got the best of everything.

The best rehab, the best prosthetics . . . My community pulled me back home and said they wanted to help me build my home. My church, my immediate family, and my extended ones were right there. Since I was the only 'wounded warrior' in my town, I got all the attention the community and town could pour out."

John's reentry was a stark contrast. "There are many more like me. I was treated for a week after the bomb and sent back to my unit. Despite the mental issues I was having, I was physically fine, and when they asked me what I wanted to do and I told them I wanted to go back to the unit, they let me do just that." John epitomized the reality of so many of our troops who are dealing with PTSD and traumatic brain injury not simply when they get home but while they are still in theater.

"And when I got home, I got off the plane, there was no processing, no parade, no nothing. I left my bags sitting outside the supply room door. There was nobody there. I got in my car and went home. I don't know that [anyone around me] ever understood, but they could see I looked different, acted different. My demeanor was different. I spent two weeks on my couch. I didn't leave. I understood that things were different, but it was only different to me. Not my wife, my mom, or my kids. That's the thing. Most of the public doesn't get to see the transformation before and after the war. Those that are close to you are most affected by the change. The family can choose to support or abandon."

John refers to traumatic brain injury, or TBI, as the signature injury of the Iraq and Afghanistan wars. "We didn't know how to test for or protect against it," John says. "The VA would give you a blood test to check for certain enzymes right after an IED, but there's no Purple Heart for a nonphysical injury. We didn't know we might have an injury. We didn't know what the risks were. We weren't told. We weren't properly prepared."

His first TBI test was a ridiculously simple two-page long assessment, something a two-year-old could do—identify the square or the circle. Now, seven years later, John has taken multiple tests that continue over several days. "I think they know more about what to look and test for. It's improving, but the general public doesn't know how to differentiate. They only know what a wounded soldier looks like—some soldier with his legs shot off."

Instead of dealing with a physical injury, John wrestles with everything that's in his head. These aren't images from the war; the war is actually still raging in his mind. "It's like all of sudden you can see all the detail like I've been trained to do. Riding down the highway at sixty miles an hour and all of a sudden I saw all the trash on the side of the road. It was always there, but I see it now because I'm conditioned to look at everything as a potential threat.

"Every person around, I log their face and look for intent. Why are they coming at me? Why are they riding my bumper? I'm going ten miles per hour above the speed limit and you got a lane wide open next to you. Why are you riding my tail? It's an intrusion of my space. The way I look at space has been shaped by my experiences."

John faced hurdle after hurdle. When he went back to work, he found himself seething with resentment and anger. He was twenty-seven years old, a veteran of Iraq, who spent his days building luxury housing for people whose values stuck in his craw. "I became very disenchanted with people who didn't respect the value that they had. They didn't respect that the people and culture are more important than material things.

"Dale had the better reintegration experience. I saw it because we were close friends and I was able to discuss that with him," says John. "When he came back there was a big party at his house. Dale played with his band, 21 Outlaw—he's the best no-legged drummer in the state—and there was a big barbecue. I remember he said, 'Wow, all these people come together and do this for me. Why me? These injuries have been happening for generations.'"

The answer was as simple as Dale's injuries being plainly visible. John, Dale says, had a tougher time because no one could see just how wounded he was.

Nobody empathized with John, nobody except Dale. Dale says that while his community was building him up, he was watching his friend slowly become disenchanted and depressed. They'd fought together. They'd bled together. And Dale realized they needed each other now more than ever. In a flash of inspiration, Dale told John he needed his help to build homes for vets. He wanted to give John a sense of purpose, belonging. He wanted them to serve together, and simultaneously help each other, the way they always had. And Purple Heart Homes has been John's salvation.

Now in its fourth year, Purple Heart Homes (PHH) was launched from three hundred square feet in the crowded printing plant that the organization still calls home. Dale and John, both drawing compensation from the VA (Dale's brings in more) kicked in a grand total of $16,000 to get PHH off the ground. They give each other mutual credit, with John saying that the inspiration is Dale— his "optimal reintegration experience" and his honed leadership skills. Dale points to John—his analytical astuteness, his practical expertise, and his "let's get this done" enthusiasm.

They are building their nonprofit with cold logic, hot passion, and real success. It started with one small act in 2009. They met Matthew Brown, a Vietnam vet with multiple injuries, PTSD included, that left him pretty much a prisoner in his own home. He needed a ramp for his wheelchair. After doing a background check to make sure he was an honorably discharged vet, the two set to work. It was seamless. And they were repaid a millionfold by the change they saw in Brown.

They're talking about Brown in the offices when, with an eerie telepathic unity, they exclaim, "Let's go visit him." One quick phone call later, John jumps into his truck and speeds off. Dale races to the car belonging to a visitor with long strides of his shiny metal legs. He slides behind the wheel, pushes the seat back as far as it will go—he's a big, big man—puts the pedal to the metal, and fishtails it out of the gravel parking lot in front of the printing plant.

He chats the whole way, talking about the PHH mission. Veterans of some wars and engagements, especially Vietnam, don't get the same medical treatment or benefits as those of the Afghanistan and Iraq conflicts, and they don't get the respect offered to World War II or Korea vets. Beyond the bricks and mortar, PHH is stimulating communities to change the way they think about veterans and to step up and take responsibility for what happens to vets in their own areas. When there's full community engagement, that's when PHH sees its best outcomes.

Dale, like John, wanted to take care of people in the worst situations, "those who have fallen through the cracks. We knew that the VA, the government were missing the gist of what it was about. That's what drove us to create PHH. We can adapt, figure out how to do it better. Yes, there was a major intimidation factor being just two country boys from North Carolina. But I went to John and said, 'You're a builder—how do we do this?' We have all kinds of soup kitchens, welfare drives. But what do people really need? A place to be safe, secure, and function, and that's their home."

Nearing Matthew Brown's house, Dale says, "We didn't know what effect we could have. When we put that deck and ramp on his house, we gave that guy a proper reintegration forty years after the fact."

Dale pulls into the driveway of a neat single-story house and walks up the deck to the front door. Brown and John are waiting. Stepping inside, John inspects the work that's been done on the house since the ramp. Brown, grizzled and limping around with the help of a cane, shows off the kitchen with its easily accessible counters and cabinets. He ushers his guests with true pride to the bathroom, with its wide, wheelchair-friendly doors. His affection, respect, and admiration for both John and Dale are in plain evidence. "These guys are amazin', just amazin'. What they did for me . . ."

The house is neat as a pin, everything arranged to accommodate Brown's disabilities. But what's really valuable is the prodding he gets from John to make sure the lawn is cleaned up, that his bills are paid on time, and that he gets out into the world. He vows to step up his game.

As we leave, John leans close to the visitor tagging along and mentions, sotto voce, that Brown's PTSD is a big factor in his reintegration—he gets shaken easily or finds it really hard to make himself leave the house sometimes. "For Matthew, it was a new-found relationship that he could be part of if he wanted to. If it was speaking to a local group, he'd get up and say, 'Here's a couple of vets that did something for me and they don't even know me.' I think he found a lot of value in that.

"When we get home, we need to feel accepted. That's what we need. I think we put that housing component in there because that's what we all desire. Whether you've been in Iraq, Iwo Jima, or Vietnam, all you can think about is getting home. It's the central hub. We believe the community believes that as well."

One at a time, John and Dale grab Brown's hand to say goodbye. He pulls both of the young veterans into an embrace, and they hug tightly. A sincere "thank you" escapes Brown's lips.

"Thank *you*," John responds.

4

■ ■ ■ ■ ■ ■ ■ ■ ■ ■

The Lesson of the Public Servant

*The Work of the People,
by the People, for the People*

"After spending so much time in finance and the military, why do you feel that now is the time to try working with the federal government?"

Margaret Dunning, a senior public relations executive at Widmeyer Communications and commissioner for the White House Fellows Program, was my interrogator, and asked the question with her signature mix of genuine curiosity and intimidating intensity. She was a petite five foot four, but her presence loomed larger.

I'd figured this question would come. It was the obvious one, and in the years since I'd graduated from college, I'd spent more time than I cared to remember in office and conference rooms, answering just these sorts of questions from committees and recruiters. In some ways, learning to answer large, abstract, existential questions with pinpoint concision and convincing logic was the skill that brought together my experiences in the corporate, academic, government, and military worlds thus far, and I was getting better at it. The fact that this skill, of all things, had turned out to be so useful told me something about my travels through the meritocracy—because the key to answering questions meant to get at who you are was to first consider *who the questioner wanted you to be*. The real answers, the ones that require genuine soul mining and a quieted mind—quiet enough to hear your own internal voice—were probably too strange or diffuse or naively idealistic to make sense in the ambient light of a conference room. The last thing you wanted to do was confuse your interviewer while scaring yourself.

But when Margaret asked me that question, I had an answer prepared and sculpted, one that talked about the need to see how leadership operated at this level of our government and how I'd long ago come to believe that public service was service in its highest form. I had practiced that answer. I knew it would come up at least a half dozen times as I worked my way through layers of approvals. I'd practiced my delivery, too. I knew when to show emotion, when to pause, when to inflect. I was prepared.

But for some reason, when I opened my mouth to begin, I froze.

The room we sat in was in Washington, D.C., in the main boardroom of one of the top law firms in the world. Large windows offered a breathtaking view of buildings that were as majestic and nearly as old as the republic. The office building was planted in the shadows of the White House, Capitol Hill, and the Supreme Court, and the view was a constant visual reminder of how close we were to the pinnacle of political power. How I answered these questions would determine whether I'd be able to take my place there.

The White House Fellows program has been around for nearly fifty years—President Lyndon Baines Johnson established the Commission on White House Fellowships in 1965. After surviving the competitive acceptance process, Fellows spend a year working full-time with a cabinet-level secretary, senior White House staff member, or another top-ranking government official. The purpose of the fellowship is to allow young, promising leaders from all walks of life the experience of government service, with the promise that they'd then go back to their own communities with new tools, ideas, and connections. President Johnson believed that "a genuinely free society cannot be a spectator society," and every administration since has supported the initiative.

Government work has something of a bad reputation, as do other kinds of traditional service work, which are seen as old-fashioned, corrupt, and inefficient. The sexy work for people who want to devote their lives to service is in the for-profit and non-profit worlds, not in the world of government.

There's an understandable reason for this. Government *can be* corrupt and inefficient, but it's still the single largest entity in our lives whose mandate is to serve the people. If used competently and effectively, government can create large-scale change in the lives of its constituents. I made my foray into the world of our enormous government with the intention of understanding whether it was true that it was a powerful entity that cared little for the lives of the people it governed, or whether there was a way to make the government work for us by choosing to work for the government. But in order to figure all this out, I first had to get the job.

■ ■ ■

At the time of my interview, I was only weeks home from Afghanistan. I ended up submitting my application while in a SCIF on the border of Afghanistan and Pakistan. I prepared my final essays days after I learned a colleague and friend of mine, First Sergeant Tobias Meister from Tulsa, Oklahoma, had been killed by a roadside bomb in Asadabad, one of the most dangerous areas of the country at the time. The most terrifying aspect of warfare, particularly asymmetric warfare, is the arbitrary and random nature of casualties. Every time you left the wire, you felt that old fatalism—the idea that there was nothing you could do about the randomness of war. Going on offensive missions was in many ways the easiest of those trips out, because we knew that on every offensive operation we were bringing overwhelming force, far greater than the target we were aiming at. But the most anxious operations were those when we were simply going from point A to point B on presumably safe journeys. The routine invited the arbitrary—there was always a chance that you just might be out there walking around a seemingly safe area when a sniper decided to take a shot at you with a twenty-year-old Russian AK-47 from four hundred yards away, or you might happen to be the unlucky soul sitting in the wrong seat in the wrong Humvee that happened to hit a mine or was rolling next to an undetected IED when it detonated. There is no preparation for that. That was the case for Meister, an amazing man whose rank of first sergeant, despite his youth, demonstrated his capacity and the admiration others had for him.

So I was already in a bad way when I got a message from Dawn that my grandfather was sick with pancreatic cancer and I needed to call home as soon as I could. But it had taken days for the message to reach me, days my grandfather did not have. When I called, he could not speak. They held the phone to his ear, and I told him how much I loved him and how important he was to me. I asked him to hold on, told him I needed to see him. I told him I am the man I am because he was the man he was. I prayed with him. He never responded, but I know in my heart he heard me. The Red Cross tried to get me out of the country in time to see him before he died, but as my travel papers were getting processed, I received word he had passed away.

I took a walk around the base, trying to hold it together. In a combat zone, I could not let my soldiers see me breaking down, especially because part of what we teach and practice is how to keep your head when the unexplainable surrounds you. But I wanted to find someone whom I could hug and find consolation with. I wanted to have someone who would listen to me tell stories about my grandfather, or listen through deep breaths and heavy tears when I talked about what he meant to me. But none of us had time for that. We all had a job to do, and everyone hurt. So I kept it in.

I pushed SEND on the online application for the White House Fellowship, just days after returning home from emergency leave to bury my grandfather. He was the wisest person I knew, and while I had seen casualties and funerals that year, his death hit me harder than any others. His funeral was the first time I'd cried in over a year.

When I was in Afghanistan, I saw young people who were some of the bravest, most courageous people I have ever met die in the arms of people who loved them. Fresh out of high school with all of their full and vibrant lives seemingly ahead of them, they never made it home. Then there were the scenes at the car pool, where vehicles both prepared for and returned from missions, where I'd see a collection of soldiers hovering around a battered vehicle, heads down, while one of them took on the unenviable task of spraying down the back of a Humvee with strong hose blasts of water to rinse off the blood of a friend. But I was a leader, and I felt that in order to be heroic, I couldn't show my emotions in their rawest form.

At my grandfather's funeral, as I looked at him lying in the casket, I remembered a sermon he had often given. He liked to explain that we are all in a kind of relay race. We carry the baton as far as we can, then we pass it on. He talked about how after wandering in the desert for forty years, Moses brought the people to the banks of the river Jordan, but that was as far as God permitted Moses to go. It was Joshua who would touch the waters and make them part, Joshua who would carry the people the next length of the journey. As unfair as it seemed to me that I had lost the men in my life when I was so young—my father when I was four, my grandfather just twenty years later—there was some comfort in the sermon. My father had been my Moses, bringing me to life. Then my grandfather became my Joshua, carrying me through my childhood and teen years into adulthood. When other boys in the neighborhood got lost in the sea of drugs and violence, my grandfather parted that sea, finding a way to get me out of the Bronx and onto higher ground. "Thank you, Papa Jim," I whispered. "I love you."

But inside that casket I also saw Toby and James and countless others whom we'd memorialized in battlefield funerals. We'd assemble the soldier's boots, placing them next to each other, as if the soldier were falling in for one final formation, and erect a weapon between them, like the spine of the soldier standing at attention. On the butt of the M-4 rifle we'd rest the Kevlar helmet, goggles perched on its crown. A soldier made from weapons and gear, almost as if he or she were present for formation, awaiting orders for the next mission that would never be. Still, motionless, these tributes symbolize the troopers who stood their ground and looked after their post until the very end. They were gone, but their place in the unit would last forever. They represented our best and died in their boots.

I hadn't cried for them then because I wouldn't allow myself to cry while I was in theater. But it all came out that day, at my grandfather's funeral. My tears for all of them.

As I left the funeral I felt freer than when I'd arrived. These amazing men and women were going to rest in peace, whether I'd made peace with their deaths or not. Their lives on this earth had earned them that. But now, in mourning, I finally felt like I had the release I'd been needing for a long time.

One of the last conversations I'd had with my grandfather was about what my plans were going to be once I got back home. I told him about the White House Fellowship, and just like every time I filled him in on what I was doing, he said he was proud of me and he knew I would get it. I was not so certain, but I knew that if I was selected for the program, it would be a year well spent, that it would further guide me and prepare me for the work I was meant to do. Evidence of my grandfather's own work was everywhere at his funeral. At the time of his death, he had almost no money in his bank account, less than a thousand dollars to leave behind, but hundreds and hundreds of people came out on a rainy day in December to pay their final respects to a man who had devoted a portion of his life to helping them with theirs. And even after all he'd given to his children, wife, congregation, neighbors, colleagues in the ministry, and friends, he'd saved the lion's share of his energy, strength, and affection for my mother, my sisters, and me. He'd loved me more than I loved myself, and he'd fought for me when I'd given up.

I was still in combat when I found out I'd been selected as a finalist for the fellowship. After a year in the tightly focused world of my mission—a year of learning the tribal traditions of eastern Afghanistan—I had to start thinking, once again, about the world outside of Khost. Suddenly it was the quotidian world of American life that seemed coded and exotic. I tried to get a sense of what was happening with gas prices and Congress while simultaneously preparing to meet with local Afghan village leaders and attend area *shuras,* or leadership councils.

It was an imperfect situation for me, trying to focus on what would get me selected while never forgetting what I needed to do to keep myself and my troops alive. The priority, always, was the success of my mission and the safety of my troops. America was an abstraction a world away, while my boots kicked up the sand of Afghanistan every day. My future, of course, would be in America, but to get back there, I had to stay in the present tense. America would wait.

Now, weeks after returning back to the United States, while still getting reacquainted with my family, my friends, and my country, while still hearing the echoes of Afghan voices in my head and seeing the faces of my fellow soldiers when I closed my eyes, I had to answer Margaret's question. Why was I sure this was the right move, to spend a year in Washington and work with the government?

When the moment came to answer, my talking points died in my mouth. The truth was, I didn't know why, and suddenly that seemed to matter a great deal to me. I had stumbled—always grateful—from Oxford to finance to the army, always at the behest of others and out of a desire to do the right thing, the best thing, the unimpeachably correct thing. Prestige, financial security, duty. But coming back home from combat, sitting in this conference room at the pinnacle of American power, was maybe one moment of whiplash too many. I didn't want to walk Margaret through all of the thoughts suddenly crashing around my head; I was in a conference room, not lying on a couch. But I also didn't have the strength for an insincere punt. So I told the truth.

"You know, I don't know," I said, and it sounded just as painfully awkward as it reads. "I know I am coming off of one of the most important and life-changing experiences of my life and I want to continue serving in some way. I am not sure if this is exactly the right way. But I know in this year I hope to learn a lot and help some as well."

I was sure I'd blown the question. I looked around the conference room table and saw some confused looks, a few corner-of-the-mouth smirks, and a number of ambiguous expressions somewhere between grimace and entertained smile. It was almost as if there'd been a memo given out about how to answer that question and I had decided not to read it. But this whiff wasn't due to a lack of preparation. Nor was it from a lack of understanding the question. I was prepared and I understood. The truth was, I was still trying to better understand and appreciate my reacclimatization.

We have well over two million veterans of the Iraq and Afghanistan conflicts in this country. I'm one of them, but I don't think I fully grasped, in those weeks right after my return, how that experience changed all of us. I don't know if I ever will. I didn't see yet that it would be impossible to simply go back to being the person I was before my deployment. I wasn't broken, I wasn't irreparably damaged, but I was different.

There were many things that made the transition back from Afghanistan difficult, and frankly, it's one of these things that you can't prepare for because everybody's return is different. For many, the return back home is relatively seamless. And even for those who have a rougher transition home, there is no one single symptom or trigger. For some, it happened immediately; there were even some for whom symptoms of post-traumatic stress struck before they left the theater. For others, it took a while.

For me, I had a lot of difficulty with lights, which came as a surprise. I had lived with 100 percent light security for a year, with nothing but little red and green flashlights after dark. To go from 100 percent light security for a year to suddenly being in Times Square can throw your brain for a loop.

No one I was around back in the States had much of an idea of what my life had been like over there, and I could sense that even when people were curious, they were also anxious about what stories I'd tell or what trauma I'd reveal. So many family members and friends vacillated between asking questions to satisfy their curiosity and express their love and concern and not asking anything out of fear of triggering some traumatic memory. This wasn't just my experience, I would find out, but was shared by almost all of my fellow soldiers. So, stuck in this enigmatic zone, many of us reverted to silence on the issue, driven by the belief that not discussing it would be the best way to return the situation to a semblance of normalcy.

I was proud of my service and the service of my fellow soldiers. I wanted to share it, spread it, celebrate it. I wanted to share the funny times we'd had, laugh about how bad our Kevlar helmets had smelled after a few months. (Especially mine. Once, after a mission I'd felt myself getting light-headed as our Black Hawk attack helicopter approached the FOB. Feeling the need to throw up, and since this was an attack helicopter and not an American Airlines 747 with barf bags resting patiently in the magazine holders in front of our seats, I simply took off my Kevlar and used it to catch my breakfast from hours earlier.) I wanted to remember out loud how we'd run half naked to the HESCOs (sand-filled reinforcements) during rocket attacks, Specialist Zuk scurrying out with nothing more than a flak vest and boxer shorts, and hear laughter through the sound of mortar explosions. When people made references to television shows like *Family Guy* and *The King of Queens,* I wanted to tell them that I'd learned about those shows from soldiers with scratchy pirated DVDs purchased from local Afghans who always managed to get their hands on the newest films and shows.

I missed hanging out with Chief Green, a Barbadian U.S. Army chief warrant officer with seventeen years of experience and three deployments under his belt. With a handsome face and chiseled frame, he looked as though he was in his early twenties, hiding the close to forty years of life he possessed. He bragged about the fact that he'd never had to leave the wire during this deployment and how, after being deployed so long and having seen as much combat as he had, not being shot at was a daily victory.

I wanted to share the fact that during target practice with members of my civil affairs team, I accidentally let off a round while trying to reholster my weapon, coming inches from shooting myself in the foot. Captain Patton, the extraordinary head of the Task Force Devil civil affairs team and a Texan through and through, played it cool, but as we were walking back from the range, he pulled me aside and through a huge smile said, "After the stuff we've seen out here, it would be pretty ironic to have to give you a Purple Heart for shooting yourself."

I wanted to talk about it all without pretext or explanation, just telling a story—specific and human—about a strange and intense period of my life. I did not want to have to set the stage for every account, have to add caveats to every anecdote, or look on with frustration as other people responded to this very intimate and personal account with an empty glance that said, *Well, I guess you had to be there.* But, of course, the most common questions I received from people when I got back were, "Did you ever kill anybody?" and "Wait, there is still fighting going on over there?"

In contrast, during the White House Fellowship process, I was struck by the depth and complexity of the questions I received from the commissioners and the other finalists: "What will you miss most about being over there?" "Is our policy currently consistent with our aims?" "Is the current Afghan leadership up to the task of being a reliable partner?" "What is Afghan food like?" "Are you doing all right since coming back?" I was finally able to start talking it through with people who seemed genuinely curious.

I'd spent that weekend with my fellow finalists being grilled with questions for eight hours a day and then monitored for the rest of the time we were awake. It was exhilarating. I was challenged and entertained. I joyfully agreed and respectfully disagreed with some of the brightest people I have ever had the pleasure of being around. I spoke about inequities in the juvenile justice system with the person who was in charge of the system in Florida. I discussed the implications of No Child Left Behind, President Bush's landmark educational legacy, with a public school teacher in northern Virginia. I discussed the public health cost implications of obesity with a cardiologist from Harvard, and energy security with a Navy SEAL. It was the most interesting few days I'd had in a long time. I felt my horizons—so recently narrowed—suddenly widening again. And I felt my relationship to the idea of government shifting once again. After my time working for the government as a soldier, I reacquainted myself with the possibilities of government as a force for good beyond its awesome capacity as a force in war and security.

And as we spent time together, the other candidates and I became friends. It reminded me of how spending time with a diverse group of motivated, service-oriented people can energize the mind and spirit like nothing else. It felt good.

Now, as I sat in that Washington boardroom in front of the commissioners, I thought quickly about all this, and before they could move on to the next question I broke in.

"I'm sorry, I just want to follow up on Margaret's last question. I'm not sure if it's about Washington, but I am excited to contribute and to be challenged again. The other finalists here have solidified in my mind why I am here and why now is the time to try serving from the standpoint of federal government."

I wasn't sure the cleanup helped my cause, but a week later I was notified that the President of the United States had just signed off on the 2006–7 class of White House Fellows and my name was on that list. Within weeks, Dawn, now my fiancée, and I were making plans to move back to Baltimore for my year as the White House Fellow to the State Department and United States Agency for International Development (USAID).

■ ■ ■

The opportunity to expand our own intellectual, spiritual, and so-cial horizons is something that can get lost when we're thinking about the next move in our lives—but it can be the most transfor-mative thing about any work we do. I'd had a couple of different modes of social experience at that point in my life. Some had been monocultures, like finance and the military, where you spend vir-tually all of your time with a group of people who have been con-ditioned with the same values, who have all had the same or very similar training, and who work with the same basic tools to exe-cute their missions. In others, like Oxford, you'd find people with different disciplinary interests, different political ideas, and differ-ent ideas about the best tools and approaches to problem solving, although less diverse in terms of social class. In the military I met people from all over the United States from all kinds of racial and social class backgrounds who had all bought into the unifying cul-ture of discipline that the military demands. At Oxford I met peo-ple from all over the world who were encouraged to tackle the world's problems from whatever angle they chose. In both cases, I gained an invaluable collateral education from the people I met—I learned how people in Georgia danced differently from people in New York, and how economists thought differently about markets than anthropologists did. This is one of the great potentials when we seek out our work in life—the potential to find fellow travelers who will join our struggle, whatever it is, lending expertise but also deepening our understanding of people all over the globe. We may set off to find our work, and end up discovering the world.

■ ■ ■

I first walked into the State Department on September 3, 2006, at
7:00 A.M. The building lacked the august architectural pomp of the
other Washington landmarks, and it was all the way across town
from the White House in a city where proximity generally ran par-
allel to importance. But none of that really mattered. It was the
State Department. I proudly placed my badge on the scanner and
smiled as the tubular metal divider lowered and allowed me access.
I was where I belonged. At least that's what my badge told me.

Because of my military and financial background, it had already
been determined before I even received my office space which
projects I was going to work on. The State Department has close to
twenty thousand employees and a budget of $27 billion for its own
operations, plus close to $50 billion for foreign aid and assistance.
Their responsibilities cover every corner of the earth.

The $50 billion in foreign aid amounted to less than 1 percent
of the federal budget (even though in surveys many Americans
guess foreign aid is more like 5–10 percent of the United States'
GDP), but it was still a significant amount, used to support those
in need and to reward good stewardship. It was also to establish
connections with the leaders and citizens of other nations, nations
that in turn became our allies, partners, friends. Other nations
have embraced the need for strong foreign aid policies as an important complement to foreign and economic policy. For example,
China in 2001 issued $1.7 billion in foreign aid; in 2011, that sum
jumped to a staggering $189.3 billion. I do not know many who
would argue that pure altruism was the only motivation behind
such a massive increase.

The challenge we had was that up until recently, there was no
way of establishing accountability for the money, no way of deter-
mining which money was being spent wisely and which money

was being wasted. The example that Secretary of State Condoleezza Rice always gave was of Haiti, which over the course of the Bush administration had received more than $1 billion in aid from the United States. As she used to say, "I would love to see, quantitatively, how that aid has been used besides the beautiful new gold-plated buildings in Port au Prince." But it was impossible to track the money.

It was this challenge that created the State Department's Office of U.S. Foreign Assistance Resources, or F Bureau, focused on foreign aid. That is where I would spend the next year of my life.

The bureau's collection of political appointees, career Foreign Service officers, and State Department employees always led to a fascinating collision of views, opinions, and timelines. For instance, each internal team generally had a certain number of political appointees, that is, supporters and friends of the administration who had excelled in other areas before deciding to spend time in government. These people operated with a ticking clock in their heads—they understood their expiration date was, at the latest, when the administration they worked for came to an end. They were in the minority of the employees there, but they usually had oversized authority and access.

The vast majority of employees I worked with were the career employees, the ones who, whether they'd been there two years or thirty years, were devoted to the State Department itself, not the politics of any specific administration. Regina was one of those career employees. She'd first come to Washington during the Ford administration, transplanting herself from South Carolina, and was now a seasoned Washingtonian who could be trusted for recommendations on the best places to grab a good meal. Never losing her southern accent or her love of grits, she also taught me the lesson of appreciating history while trying to change it. She had seen multiple administrations, from both parties, come in thinking they could change an entire structure in a year; they always ended up becoming frustrated and disgruntled within months. Moving the deep bureaucracy of lifelong civil servants was more like steering a tanker than a speedboat. "Have a few priorities, a few things you are willing to stake everything on, and get those things done," she told me. "If you have ten priorities, you have no priorities."

As a fellow, I was on an even tighter timeline than the political appointees whose alarms went off every four years. The experiences of all the fellows were different, but one fact held true: our time there was finite, and, since we were not political appointees, it was up to us to define the type of experience we had. Three hundred and sixty-five days from our first day, we would be replaced. Somebody new would walk in with the same inexperience and naïveté. The faster we realized this fact, the better the experience went.

One of the things I sought out was a chance to shift my perspective on the war I'd just left. A problem with the debates about our foreign policy in Washington is that very few people there have ever taken the pulse of what's happening on the ground thousands of miles away. I became friends with Alonzo Fulgham at USAID, who would eventually become its chief administrator. He'd started his international career as a Peace Corps volunteer in Haiti, and decades later his career included fascinating jobs such as foreign service officer in Azerbaijan and Jordan, USAID mission director in Afghanistan, and the first-ever chief operating officer of USAID. His smile and bow tie were constants, as were the piercing questions he posed in briefings. He was always curious to hear my opinion about Afghanistan and what it was like for the ground soldiers over there fighting. Alonzo would ask me, "So how are we doing?"—referring to how we were doing at closing the stubborn disconnect between those who made policy and those whose job it was to implement it.

"We're doing well, but this challenge is . . . um, multitiered," I replied.

Alonzo smiled. "Ah, multitiered, which is a code word for 'There is something I want to say but can't.' Kind of like when people say 'That's interesting' about something that really isn't."

I chuckled because he was right, but then I tried to explain how I really felt. Afghanistan was definitely more of a priority in Washington than I'd thought while over in the country fighting. The number of thoughtful people we had working on the issue was admirable. But the complexity of the mission—a mission devised in Washington but executed on the ground in Afghanistan by service people and diplomats—was not always fully reckoned with in D.C. The connection between the people making the policy and the people on the ground can get lost.

Working in the international arena offers up some special challenges. Policy makers who focus on domestic issues, the ones that directly affect the American people, who are both our constituents and our funders, can see and even put their hands on the results of the work they do. A new bridge gets built, a hospital is repaired, a social program is preserved. They get it. But work overseas is different. For instance, the government can be doing great work internationally: getting aid to people in need, responding to disasters, supporting regimes that do well by their citizens and shedding light on those that leave their citizens in the dark. But the vast majority of Americans would have no idea. They don't see it. It's only when bad things happen, some of which are completely out of our control, that the drumbeat begins to be heard in the American media. And even when things go right, the massive indifference of the American public can sometimes shift into resentment over the amount of resources being spent. Some people would prefer that fewer—or none—of our resources ever leave this country at all.

This is a tricky point to navigate. Why should we care about what's going on thousands of miles away? Afghanistan was an exceptional issue, you might think: here was a country whose instability and takeover by radicals had led almost directly to attacks on our own soil. And yet before long Americans became fatigued by stories from Afghanistan and the ever-growing number of American casualties. We became frustrated by the slow progress of the country's developments toward democracy and stability. Afghanistan, despite its importance and our responsibility for its predicament, quickly started to seem like a sinkhole.

If we are impatient about an exceptional case such as Afghanistan, then how much more impatient will we be when our efforts are driven more by humanitarianism and compassion than self-interest and security? Even when you talk to aid workers or workers at nonprofits whose philanthropic work takes them overseas, they will tell you that Americans ask them: *Why don't you just focus your work on America? Why go to Africa or Asia or South America to help kids or help with disasters? Why not do it right here?*

There are complicated answers to these questions, and working in the State Department only began to help me understand them. I'm not a warmonger—like many who have worn the uniform, I am particularly averse to war. I'm also not someone who believes in empire building or imperialistic or paternalistic attitudes about the world outside of America. But our passion, influence, and responsibility as humans can never end at our borders.

Of course, the United States has an imperative role to play around the world. History and our share of the world's resources have given us jobs as friend, funder, enforcer, cajoler, peacemaker, peacekeeper, supporter, healer, and leader all at once—and this applies both to our government and to our nonprofit and nongovernmental organizations. This work can be justified through pure self-interest, the simplest formulation of which is this: We live in an interconnected world. We can't hide in our own country while the world around us explodes. Everything from terrorism to epidemics to environmental crises affects all of us, even if it's happening on the other side of the world. That's the crudest case for America's engagement internationally—and for the urge many individuals and nonprofits feel to commit to work overseas. But then there's the moral case that goes beyond the actions of governments. Humanity is borderless. Compassion is universal.

In his brilliant "Letter from Birmingham City Jail," Dr. Martin Luther King, Jr. expressed a similar sentiment. After he, Fred Shuttlesworth, Ralph Abernathy, and other civil rights leaders were imprisoned for leading a peaceful march against segregation in Birmingham, Alabama, they received a newspaper with an op-ed entitled "A Call for Unity." The op-ed was penned by a group of Alabama clergy who deplored the actions of the jailed civil rights leaders as "unwise and untimely." Dr. King and his team were called "outside agitators" and told that their actions were actually detrimental to the progress of the movement. Dr. King decided to respond to the clergy's opinion piece, taking on each of their points with a poignancy and clarity that made his letter one of the most important documents in American history. Responding to accusations of being an "outsider" (by virtue of his being from Mont-gomery, not Birmingham), he wrote:

> But more basically, I am in Birmingham because injustice is here. Just as the prophets of the eighth century B.C. left their villages and carried their "thus saith the Lord" far beyond the boundaries of their home towns, and just as the Apostle Paul left his village of Tarsus and carried the gospel of Jesus Christ to the far corners of the Greco Roman world, so am I compelled to carry the gospel of freedom beyond my own home town. . . . Injustice anywhere is a threat to justice everywhere. We are caught in an inescapable network of mutuality, tied in a single garment of destiny. Whatever affects one directly, affects all in-directly.

The huge challenges the globe faces can be met only if we're all pulling together, if we can make use of all of the world's human resources. And for people driven by religious or secular ethics, it's hard to argue that the needs of Americans are somehow more im-portant than the needs of people anywhere else in the world. The question is, *What need can I best help address?* For some of us, we can do our best work in our own homes and communities; others of us are called to do work in other parts of the world. The oppor-tunity to help is not limited by borders—and the beautiful part is that when we reach our hands across the globe to serve others, we don't return empty-handed. There is always an exchange. I learned that from Abdullah. And I would learn it again during my fellow-ship.

■ ■ ■

Every other day during the fellowship, the fellows would gather for lunch with interesting people who'd made their careers in government, the nonprofit sector, business, or some combination of them all, and would share their lessons about life, leadership, and service with us. The tempo of the lunches and meetings was aggressive: a week's schedule might include lunch with former General Electric CEO Jack Welch on Monday, former commander of U.S. forces in Afghanistan and CIA head General David Petraeus on Wednesday, and Virginia governor Mark Warner (who eventually went on to become the senior senator for the commonwealth), wrapping up the week.

The most memorable meeting was in the Oval Office with the president, who spent an hour and a half speaking with the entire class. Many of us left that office with a very different perspective on a man whom we all knew from television but no closer. The depth with which he spoke about the issues—and the kindness and sincerity with which he answered each of our questions—was impressive, even on issues where I remained unpersuaded. But as we left, what was on most of our minds was probably the fact that we had all *just met with the president in the Oval Office.* I walked out of the West Wing next to my friend Chris. Chris was one of the six fellows—out of eleven altogether—with at least one parent who was born in another country. I was another. Chris's parents had fled Cuba for the United States in 1969.

"How do you feel?" I asked him as we started moving toward the White House gates.

He sighed deeply. "Overwhelmed," he said finally, then fell silent again.

■ ■ ■

In addition to international trips to India and China, there were also domestic trips included in our fellowship. It was our first domestic trip, to Mississippi and Louisiana, that most impressed me.

Jackson, Mississippi, was the first stop on this domestic policy tour. The purpose of the tour was not to conduct a seminar on race relations, but race was the subtext of every conversation. In many respects I found it refreshing. I was accustomed to living with the subtleties of race and racism every day but never being able to talk frankly about it. Conversations about race unearth fear, frustrations, and embarrassments as old as the republic, so many people choose not to talk about it at all, as if silence will make our problems vanish. We cower, similar to the way toddlers cover their eyes under the false assumption that since they cannot see us, we cannot see them either. But in Mississippi, race was on the table, every table, in almost every interaction. For some northerners, the South is where racism happens. It was the South that launched the Civil War in defense of slavery. It was in the South that, even after the brutal death grip of institutionalized slavery was lifted, Jim Crow came to life. It was to Arkansas that President Eisenhower had to send the 82nd Airborne—the very group I'd just been fighting with in Afghanistan—to protect a young black girl who wanted to attend school. It was Alabama that gave us images of Bull Connor siccing dogs on defenseless protestors and allowing police officers to turn fire hoses on children. It was in Mississippi that Dr. King spoke of the "sweltering heat of injustice." It was the South that voted en masse for the presidential candidate who promised "segregation forever." It is also four southern states, Mississippi, Arkansas, Alabama, and Georgia, that honor the Confederate flag or a version of the Southern Cross within their state flags.

But then again, I could make another list—from race riots to busing controversies to race-based ghettoized housing policy to complicity in the slave trade—showing that race issues are hardly exclusive to the South. The refreshing thing I found in Mississippi was that in the South, the reality of race is not ignored or hidden or euphemized away. While northerners can offload the nation's guilt over racism on the South, in the South they have to face it head-on—there's no place to bury it. It's theirs to live with, for better or worse.

When we went down to Mississippi, we met with Reverend Weary, an older African American clergyman, who explained to us how when he left the South to go to college, he had no desire to ever return to a place that was so full of memories of hatred and vicious discrimination. He remembered vividly when blacks could not drink from the same water fountain as whites, or could not even sit down on a bus without first thinking about how their seat selection would be interpreted by others. Though he'd been in a rush to leave Jackson, he ended up spending decades more there, working to address the legacy of the racism that had shaped his upbringing. He decided to come back to Jackson to be part of changing his home, and not just joining the chorus of distant complainers and detractors. I respected his choice, and that of so many others we met on that trip, who argued that the future of Mississippi and our nation requires us to address problems, not act as if they don't exist. At that moment I thought about my old friend Abdullah and our conversations about race. I wished he could have met Reverend Weary. Our national path was jagged, but our progress was significant. What Reverend Weary shared with us was in many ways connected directly with the struggle Abdullah was forging thousands of miles away. Discomfort wasn't the enemy; stalemate was.

This is another key to finding your life's work. One of the things I discovered when I wrote my first book was that no matter how much I wanted to tell my story, there were still aspects of it that I felt uncomfortable talking about. But I pushed myself to tell it all as honestly as possible; to use a cliché, I pushed myself beyond my comfort zone. When I talk to people who've read my first book, I find that the stories around which I felt the most discomfort—those involving my own failures, dishonesty, and fear—were the ones readers connected most powerfully with. It was in the uncomfortable places that I'd found my catharsis—a breakthrough—and it was in reading about that discomfort that others were able to connect to their own moments of discomfort and find their own breakthroughs. The same applies to the dilemma of many returning vets that I talked about before. Sometimes we want to pretend that we didn't see the things we saw over there, or feel the things we felt: panic, despair, heartbreak, guilt. But when vets get together in a safe space and bare their souls, they find freedom from the things that haunt them.

The same is true when it comes to finding the work that matters to you. Sometimes we can find our work in the larger world—in faraway places with a burning need. But sometimes, like Reverend Weary, we find it in the place we thought to run from. The biblical story of Jonah is a familiar and apt metaphor for how we find our work—or how our work finds us. When we run to the thing we fear, the problem that keeps us up at night, sometimes we find the work we were meant to do all along. When it comes to race in America, I hope that one day we, as individuals and as a country, run right into that scary place and free ourselves of its burden at last.

As much as the word "race" underlined our first domestic policy trip, there was another word that dominated our experience even more: Katrina. We were heading to the Gulf Coast just two years after that hurricane slammed into Mississippi and Louisiana. The hurricane and its aftermath were responsible for the deaths of at least eighteen hundred people. Two years later, the region remained devastated.

On our second day in the area, we visited a classroom in the Bay St. Louis School District in Mississippi. The educational system there was challenged even prior to Katrina. According to the Annie E. Casey Foundation, even before the storm, Mississippi and Louisiana were battling it out as the states with the forty-ninth and fiftieth lowest-performing public school districts in the country. Race was again a major factor: 67 percent of the population of Jackson, Mississippi, was black, for instance, but 97 percent of the public school population was black. Whites in Mississippi had fled the public schools in response to federal mandates for integration and had never returned. But while the flaws in their system were obvious, I was more impressed by the intense focus of the community to make sure that these kids—who had every imaginable obstacle placed in their path—had a chance to succeed.

These efforts were led by one of our own, a White House Fellow named Jason Dean who had worked with the state government, coordinated volunteers in the aftermath of the hurricane, and assisted educational groups in getting funding to recover from the damage of the storm. Jason, with his sandy brown hair and cozy southern drawl, had an affability that masked a strong passion for results. He was a native Mississippian and served as our de facto tour guide during the trip to the Gulf. Bay St. Louis was one of the areas that had been utterly destroyed during the storm. Whole neighborhoods had been wiped out, houses now replaced by a sea of Federal Emergency Management Agency trailers. Trailers also served as classrooms and as mental health facilities, where ailments and obstacles ranging from depression to asbestos inhalation to child abuse were diagnosed and dealt with.

During our tour, we had the chance to meet with a group of fourth graders. They had been told we were from the White House, and smiles and looks of awe beamed from their beautiful faces. Maybe they thought we were there to help. Maybe they thought we were there to announce the coming of brand-new school buildings, chalkboards, school materials. Maybe they were just excited that somebody from as far away as the White House even knew they existed. Jason led our class discussion with them.

Most of the kids we met were soaking wet and had their shoes off. We found it curious, but the school superintendent explained that they were currently experiencing a series of terrible storms and most of the kids had gotten soaked walking through epic puddles on their way to school. So we stood at the front of the classroom with a group of drenched children staring up at us. Tears literally welled up in Jason's eyes as he began the discussion by asking, "How many of you slept in trailers last night?"

At least three-quarters of the hands shot in the air.

"How many of you were scared by the storms last night?"

All of the hands went in the air. Kids started describing to us what the storms were like. In excited voices, they talked about thunder so loud it felt like it was ripping through the trailers and flashes of lightning that lit their rooms up like it was midday.

"I had a hole that was leaking water on my head," said one.

"Me too, and I felt like I was going to get pushed in the water!" another yelled out.

The kids were sleepless, wet, and still dealing with haunting memories of destruction that will likely stay with them for the rest of their lives, yet here they were this morning, ready to learn. They had no idea how their presence inspired us.

Chris asked the kids a question. "Do you all know what a hero is?"

A wide range of answers echoed through the double-wide trailer.

"Someone who helps people."

"Someone who fights bullies."

"Someone in the army."

Chris listened to their answers and responded in a soft voice.

"All those are good answers. But you all are our heroes."

We didn't come down to that school district bearing gifts that would transform their lives, alas. We came to bear witness to what poverty, isolation, and natural disaster had wrought on their lives and to leave with a broader understanding of the work that needed to be done. But, as often happens, we left inspired by the way that people on the ground in that storm-ravaged country were, on their own, by their own will, making a way. The nature of service is always reciprocal: you can go into a project thinking that you are in some way helping others, but of course you end up helping yourself, if only by being reminded that every day people in all kinds of circumstances all over the world get up and find a way through them.

The rest of the week was no less important to our growth and development. We spent time with government leaders and community organizers. We met with corporate executives fighting to keep jobs in the area, and with local musicians who stayed and played, inspired by a new sense of purpose and motivation. We spent one night at a glamorous reception at the top of the One Shell Place Building, the tallest building in New Orleans, and then in the morning headed to the Lower Ninth Ward, ground zero for the death and destruction.

This was my second exposure to the Lower Ninth Ward. My first had come just weeks after I arrived back from Afghanistan. I had heard about the storm while I was in Afghanistan, but at the time I hadn't fully appreciated the destruction and aftermath. It was not until I came back to the United States that I understood the level of the devastation. This storm affected ninety thousand square miles of the Gulf Coast—an area roughly the size of the United Kingdom. And the Lower Ninth Ward was the most well-documented area of the destruction. It was not simply the storm that caused the damage. The Lower Ninth is where a hundred-yard section of levee failed, causing a tsunami-like rush of water to flood the area, with no outlet for it to drain away. My mother was doing some work down in New Orleans and asked me if I would like to go down there with her. I saw it both as a great chance for a bonding experience with my mother and as an opportunity to see firsthand the aftereffects of the storm.

What I saw, particularly when we went to the Lower Ninth Ward, was unforgettable. Homes literally sitting on top of cars. As the water receded, the smell of mold and death and emptiness filled the air. Staircases sat in solitude in open spaces that used to be residences. We walked slowly, uneasily, through the ward, at one point passing a sign that said "Tourists, shame on you. 1,600 people died here." The disturbing thought entered my mind that while I had just come back from a combat zone in a part of the world that ranked toward the bottom on every global indicator—economic, health, political, and social—the destruction I saw in the Lower Ninth Ward of New Orleans matched what I'd seen in Afghanistan, blow for blow.

With my fellowship class I returned to the same spots a year later, walked the same streets, heard the same complaints about lack of cooperation between federal, state, and local officials. Some debris had been cleaned up, some homes torn down in preparation for new ones. We got to tour the 17th Street levee and canal and the new pumping station in Lake Pontchartrain, a neighboring jurisdiction. Many NGOs were leaning in to solve some of the challenges that plagued the area. But this trip left us simultaneously well aware of the impact of human failure and inspired by the potency of the human spirit. It also reminded me of just how vital good and responsive government is—and how we can never take it for granted. Government work has been slandered in so many ways over the last generation that good people may well have been driven away from it. But there on the Gulf Coast its necessity and honor were on clear display.

Toward the end of my fellowship year, I was asked by Ambassador Henrietta Fore, who had become my boss midway through the year, about my plans and whether I was interested in staying in government. Once again I was at a crossroads, and confused. I'd come to Washington and applied to the White House Fellowship in order to learn about government. What I'd learned is that while there are some extraordinary people in our country's bureaucracy, government was far from the only way to serve others. As I sat in Ambassador Fore's office, the same office that General George Marshall sat in as he crafted the Marshall Plan, she told me about the importance of the work they were doing in the State Department. She spoke with conviction and factual authority.

But I hadn't quite figured out how to align the things I thought were important with the things I thought I could do best. I had come to have enormous respect for the work being done in terms of foreign aid in the State Department, but the life of a bureaucrat, of a government official, was one that I wasn't sure was my own.

One thing I began to realize in my travels was that everyone I met who was truly successful—whether in business, in philanthropic work, in human rights, in government, or in raising a family—shared one common trait: they were fanatically passionate about the work they did. They breathed it. They needed it. It was their lifeblood. Really, think about it: name one person in your own life who fits any description of unassailable success who is not driven by that kind of clarifying passion. As I left Ambassador Fore's office, I didn't yet feel that passion. I was once again experiencing a kind of cloudiness, bordering on frustration, about where I was in life and what I wanted to do. I went back to my office and leaned back in my chair. The front legs lifted slowly off the ground, placing pressure on the back two legs. I closed my eyes, brought my hands to my head, and rubbed my temples. The great joke Rhodes Scholars make was echoing in my head: "A Rhodes Scholar is someone who has a great career behind him."

I had to learn to trust myself, because my gut told me that all the directions I was being pulled in were not mere distractions but rather part of an eloquent design. It would take time for me to weave the pieces of my experience together, to see in the brush strokes of each place that I apprenticed in—from the offices of the State Department to the deserts of Afghanistan, from the halls of Oxford University to the trading floors of Deutsche Bank—that I was becoming the man I hoped to be.

■ ■ ■ ■ ■ ■ ■ ■ ■ ■ ■ ■ ■ ■ ■ ■ ■ ■ ■

The Globalist

ESTHER BENJAMIN
Peace Corps

"Why not devote your efforts to the place where you live, rather than trying to save the world?"

Or "Why help kids in America when there are kids in other parts of the world who suffer much more?"

I've heard people ask both questions, and there's something valid in both. There are major problems in this country that we should all be devoting our energy to solving. There's a lot of truth in the old saying that charity begins at home. But there's also truth to the notion that whatever problems we have in America pale next to the problems of people in the developing world. Even the least-advantaged people in America have better access to education, more material possessions, and a stronger safety net than perhaps the majority of people around the world. A hardcore ethicist would probably say that we shouldn't spend another dime on our own problems till we've solved the far more desperate problems of the starving, war-displaced, and profoundly impoverished people in other parts of the world.

I'm certainly not in a position to resolve the difference between these views, and that's sort of the point. Each of us has to find the place where we can do the most to help. For Esther Benjamin, that meant straddling worlds—working in public service for the United States government, but using that position to help people around the globe. We follow our work where it leads us, and the greatest tools we have are portable: our minds, our hearts, our hands. As theologian Frederick Buechner put it so beautifully: "The place God calls you to is the place where your deepest gladness, and the world's deepest hunger, meet."

"One second, Mr. Geithner. Ms. Benjamin will head in to see the president first."

Tim Geithner, the seventy-fifth secretary of the treasury of the United States, stops his quick stride toward the door of the Oval Office. The frizzy-haired cabinet secretary looks at Esther Benjamin and smiles. Esther, seated in the wooden chair next to the door at the Oval Office, smiles back. It is 2012, and the United States is in the midst of digging out of one of the most challenging five-year spans in our nation's financial history. On the agenda at that moment: a still stagnant housing market, a rising stock market offset by frustratingly high unemployment, and a looming euro zone crisis that threatens to swallow any financial progress the United States has made at getting out of what's becoming known as the Great Recession.

But that all can wait. Up next on the president's agenda is a private meeting with his forty-three-year-old associate director of the Peace Corps. She's not sure what the meeting is for. A week ago she received an invitation from the president to meet with him in his office. She's come prepared to brief him on the progress the Peace Corps has made under its director, Aaron Williams, and herself. She can talk about plans to celebrate the Corps's fiftieth year of operation. Maybe the president wants to speak about the Focus In/Train Up initiative that Esther and her team started to maximize the skills of its volunteers and provide world-class volunteer and staff training. Maybe he wants to congratulate her on the fact that the Peace Corps has now reentered Colombia, Indonesia, Nepal, and Sierra Leone. The short-term, high-impact Peace Corps Response Program has significantly expanded under Benjamin's watch, and the Corps is now providing new opportunities for medical professionals through the Global Health Service Partnership.

When she is told the president is ready for her, she rises from her seat and moves toward the door. Her brown eyes dart to the crimson curtains that frame the president's oak desk. This is not her first time in the Oval Office; she's been there before as a White House Fellow under President Clinton. But this time it's different. This is not a tour. This is a meeting with her boss.

President Obama's enormous smile greets Esther as he moves from behind the desk to shake hands. Soon Esther will realize that, rather than have her brief him on the Corps's activities, the president of the United States wants to thank Esther not only for her service but also for her story.

They talk about her family and their struggle, about her past and how that has influenced her path. Esther could be doing anything—everyone recruited Esther, and the truth is, they haven't stopped—but she chose to devote herself to government service. And now Barack Obama is sitting with her for fifteen minutes just to thank her.

"You represent the American dream, Esther," the president says proudly. He's absolutely right—and, in many ways, even more than he knows.

Esther was born on May 4, 1969, in Murunkan, Sri Lanka, a small village made up largely of her extended family of rural Tamils. Her father, Paul, was a United Methodist minister and Old Testament theologian. Her mother, Saroja, was a star athlete and college edu-cated, both anomalies in the remote northern farming region. Ed-ucated, open-minded, and inclusive, Benjamin's parents brought her up with a moral imperative to do good and give back. Service was a family tradition. Esther was raised to have a strong work ethic and to devote herself to the pursuit of justice and fairness.

These ideas of social justice and activism still drive her. Benja-min launches herself out of bed at four o'clock each morning and coasts through every day at Mach 5 speed.

"I never felt entitled to anything. No matter what I accomplish, even after having been a White House Fellow and the opportuni-ties I've had professionally, I'm grateful to work hard. Sometimes I see people as they progress and the work ethic can wane. I was up at 4:00 A.M., went for a run, polished a presentation, and pulled the senior team together. I said thank God I never feel entitled to any-thing. I don't complain for the hard work that lies before me."

That joyful relentlessness has propelled her throughout life—
that and her fearlessness. "I think just being a Tamil and my Tamil
identity make me kind of fearless," she says. Those potent traits,
coupled with her innate intellect and talent, perfectly suited her to
become associate director for global operations at the Peace Corps,
a position carved out for her at a time when the august but aging
agency was in dire need of reinvention and strong, creative, and
rational management.

Peace Corps director Aaron Williams, a close colleague, mentor,
and friend (who has since retired), asked Benjamin to come on
board. "The greatest honor," she says, "was being appointed by the
president. I'm humbled that I'm in a position where I get to send
nearly ten thousand of the most incredible Americans to serve in
very small, rural communities around the world, like where I was
born. It's a full circle. This job has been very personal from day
one. I've visited many volunteers working in exactly the types of
villages where my family lives."

At Benjamin's government-issue executive desk, the surface
clear of clutter, in her corner office in the Peace Corps building
that's bright with sun and fluorescent light, personal photos cover
every sill and shelf that isn't taken up with neatly shelved manuals,
briefing books, and other official-looking binders. The window
ledge is devoted to photos of Benjamin's two children, both bearing strong resemblances to Benjamin, with their black hair and
shining dark eyes. Santham, nine years old, whose name means
"peace," declares that he'll be president one day. Her fifteen-year-
old daughter, Anjali—her name means "to give praise"—has a
passion for design and social justice. There's one framed glossy of
the mother and kids in Paris, another at the Great Wall. Another
has all three on camelback in front of the pyramids. It's only fitting

that images of her family surround Esther every day, as so much of who she is is embedded in her family and its story.

Murunkan, the name of the village where she was born, means "one large extended family." Esther's parents are relatives, and sought parental permission to marry when Saroja was in college and Paul was in graduate school in India. "We are from an area with only one language, Tamil," says Saroja, a small woman exploding with energy and entrepreneurial spirit. "My father said that's not right, and that's why he sent us to boarding school, where we were exposed to English. . . . In Sri Lanka, if you can speak English, that means you're educated."

Paul's relationship to education is no less passionate but of different origins. "After my father died, I was considered an orphan even though my mother was still alive. The Methodist Church gave me a scholarship that went from elementary through high school, then college," says Paul. "The church has a strong tradition of caring for the fatherless. It was because of that I had the chance to go to high school, and from then on I was able to fly."

Paul finished graduate school in India, Saroja graduated from college, and in 1968 they married in a small church where Paul was pastor. Esther was born a year later, May 4, 1969. Saroja recalls there were four church placements in one year alone when Esther was a baby. With her general degree from the University of Sri Lanka, Saroja figured she ought to do something, so she started a Montessori school. Wherever Paul was pastoring, she'd start up another nursery school and teach her charges English rhymes that their parents loved to hear.

"Esther was in my nursery school," Esther's mother recounts, "but she was dreaming about going to elementary school and high school. She was dreaming about that when she was little."

Esther's sense of Tamil and family identity were forged in Murunkan. She says her fondest memories are of running barefoot through the open paddy fields from one cousin's house to the other, or sticking close to her beloved grandfather. "There was a sense in my community, a sense in my family and especially from my grandfather, that I was going to be the one of the family who would do great service. The reason I say the name of the village so much is because my identity is tied to the village where I originate from," says Esther.

Paul says that although they rarely lived in Murunkan, the village made a great impression on his daughter. "There was that openness that was always there," he says, recalling his brother feeding an enemy government soldier during wartime. Food was a human need and so it must be met, his brother said.

In 1976, Paul came to the United States to study at the University of Texas in Austin, and saved enough money during the next months to bring over Saroja and Esther. "I arrived in Austin without a word of English," says Esther. "My parents never made a big deal of our moves; they just did it. The fact that they didn't have a lot of anxiety about moves within Sri Lanka and between countries influenced how we reacted to moves. It was positive. When I got to Texas, my parents dropped me off at the Robert E. Lee Elementary School. Of course I didn't know the symbolism. Their attitude was, 'Here we are, go learn, go be.'

"I remember being disoriented because I didn't understand people. I remember being determined. I don't know exactly how long it was, but I felt within my childhood memory it was about two weeks before I was speaking English. It was complete immersion. I made friends right away. The teachers were terrific. Very shortly thereafter I was speaking English with a thick Texan accent. When we returned to Sri Lanka a year later, people who spoke English didn't believe that's what I was speaking.

"I think it was an all-white school. I certainly didn't think or speak about it in these terms, but the takeaway was that there are moments in time when we have opportunities that are vastly different than the norms in life. You have to seize every aspect of those opportunities. Don't shy away, don't retreat, don't walk away in frustration, and don't get overwhelmed. Being overwhelmed detracts from opportunity. I was seven then, and I still feel that way every day. When I'm in a room in a discussion with new people on new subjects, I think the skills of life as an ethnic minority and my experience as an American immigrant taught me not to get frustrated or overwhelmed but to make the most of it."

By 1977, when the family decided to return to Sri Lanka, hostilities between the majority Sinhalese and the Tamils were heating up. "We couldn't get back to Sri Lanka, and Paul left us in Singapore for two weeks. We were scared to death," recalls Saroja. "Then we were going by train from Colombo to Murunkan, where our parents are from, our birthplace, to see our relatives. We were holding our passports, so if something happened we could just run into the jungle. In the seventies it really flared up and never went away." For nearly three decades there would be intermittent fighting between the government and the Liberation Tigers of Tamil Eelam (LTTE), known as the Tamil Tigers, though when the conflict began nobody expected it would last as long as it did or claim the lives of close to a hundred thousand people.

Saroja says that Esther had a hard time with the homecoming.

"She forgot the language; she couldn't remember any Tamil. In the city she was okay talking in English, but even then they couldn't understand the Texan English. Paul's sister"—a university-educated botanist—"and brother-in-law couldn't understand her. So she couldn't talk to relatives, and that was hard for her. She never fully recovered that. She was able to learn some of the language back, but not really."

The family was assigned to yet another church on the east coast of the country. In 1979 a cyclone hit and destroyed their parsonage home. "Esther was really afraid. It was midnight and she asked, 'Are we going to die?' But God was with us," says Saroja. "We rebuilt the parsonage."

Soon after, Esther was sent to Colombo, the capital, to study at a Methodist boarding school. It was ethnically diverse, which was manageable but unnerving. "Things changed toward the end of the seventies. In earlier years I didn't particularly notice our identities." When she moved back to her parents' new home, though, the differences were thrown into sharp relief.

"My father was the principal of an ecumenical theological college," says Esther. "We lived on campus. There were Buddhist monks, Catholic priests, Methodists, and Baptists. I was seeing people across racial and cultural identities. But because that part of the country was predominantly Sinhala, it was quite controversial for a Tamil to be the school's head. It became increasingly tense."

Saroja calls it an "international place. We had Americans, British, the Sinhala, and Tamil-speakers. Germans and Indians came to teach. The whole seminary was up on a hill, surrounded by avocado and mango trees, banana trees, coffee, cinnamon, cardamom, a rich kind of area. We got our coconuts from coconut trees. For

Esther that childhood memory was remarkable. All the children played together until it was dark, speaking in all three languages. It was a nice time. But when they came down from the hill, it was a different world."

Esther speaks of the painful contradictions. "In school there was the Tamil medium, the Sinhalese medium. We'd come together for certain classes—music, a class on religion, and maybe for an English class. So there were three times throughout the week that we were together.

"I have a memory of a music class where the teacher said, 'The Sinhala kids can sit in the front and the Tamil can sit in the back.' I remember feeling that wasn't right. I remember the next time we had the class, I got the Tamil kids together and said, 'Let's sit in front.' We went early and sat in front. I don't think we were asked to move. But I had a real sense early on of right and wrong and a sense of social justice."

According to Esther, she understood different traditions and embraced all the kids. "I was fluent in Sinhala. There were community plays that I'd act in and I had a perfect Sinhala accent." Esther takes in a ragged breath. "This is the first time I've talked about this."

All around the family, the racial tensions flared. Says Paul, "In 1981 or '82, when we were getting ready to come back to the U.S. the second time—I was coming as part of a faculty training program to do my Ph.D.—we received information that the Sinhalese were coming to track us. At the time my Sinhala children surrounded the house to make sure we were safe."

As the situation grew increasingly untenable, Esther says, "my parents were thoughtful and strategic and decided we had to flee the country. My father had been accepted in a Ph.D. program in the U.S., and so in some ways we fled the country with great opportunity. I was thirteen years old."

Saroja and Paul sold everything, looking simply for some money to buy tickets and start over. "Until you get the visa, go to the airport, get into the plane, you're not sure. Even now, when I go back, an American citizen, I get scared sometimes of whether I'll be able to get out because of the war. We lost so many people and family members. I was hearing stories of the savagery of the war. It's all fear," Esther says. "So much of me is tied to Murunkan, and when we left I was losing a country that was just entering the civil war. I didn't think we were going to get out of Sri Lanka safely. I didn't think we'd be able to get on the plane safely or even get to the airport safely. The plane taking off was the biggest relief I ever felt. I remember my parents saying, 'We're going to America and you're going to have so many opportunities.' I felt relief, and pretty instinctively felt in my gut, 'To whom much is given, much is expected.' Many others who would have loved to did not make it out."

The plane put them down in St. Louis, where Esther completed ninth grade. Then it was on to Chicago's Hyde Park neighborhood, where her brother went to a magnet school that she remembers as "90 percent black. It was a completely different environment. But I don't walk into a place and feel like I don't belong. I was perfectly comfortable. I think I'm able to adapt so fast because I had such gratitude for the privilege of being here when I'd hear so constantly about lives being destroyed back home. I felt guilty, probably. But guilt isn't a useful emotion. [I don't want] regret, anger, all emotions that aren't useful, productive, or constructive. I always choose to recognize the privilege that I have."

She hit another major turning point when she finished high

school. Her father completed his Ph.D., and her parents decided together that he would return to Sri Lanka to resume his position as head of the theological college. Esther, her sister, and her mother stayed in the United States.

"It was very difficult. I was very close to my father. His absence was huge for me. For the next five years I saw him once or at most twice a year. It was very tough on my parents. I missed my father's presence and influence. But from that moment I further understood my family's sense of responsibility and obligation. Do what you say you're going to do. If you say you're going to get the degree and then return, that's what you do. My father is very much a man of honor, his word."

Her inclusiveness, her devotion to the Methodist tradition, and her exposure to realities outside the comfort zone of most Americans facilitated Esther's easy passage into North Central College, which she lovingly describes as a "suburban, all-white" Methodist institution. She graduated with honors in 1990. She earned a master's degree in international affairs from American University in 1992 (later earning a second in applied economics), and made a passionate commencement speech about social justice that landed her a job in Somalia as U.N. humanitarian affairs officer in 1993. It was her first job—and while most people on their first job spend their time learning the ropes and working on entry-level responsibilities, she immediately dived into famine relief issues in one of the poorest, most dire situations on earth at the time. The job exposed her to the true human devastation of war—that it is never only the soldiers who suffer. She already knew this, as she had seen it in her own childhood. But now she actually had the chance to do something about it. Her ability to step in and address the injustices she witnessed was intoxicating.

Upon completing that service, Benjamin continued to move up the government ranks. She loved government's ability to have huge, immediate impact. She loved the chance to represent something bigger than herself. The same entity that had served and protected her and her family when they needed it most was something she was now able to leverage in order to serve others. Her work was driven in part by a desire to say thank you—to repay to others what she had received.

"I'm not looking to be associated with the biggest names and titles in the world. I'm looking for the biggest ideas. The boldest innovations. I'm looking for the initiatives that touch people who are otherwise not helped. I serve this nation because I am thankful to her. She is more powerful than any physical embodiment. She is an idea, the most powerful idea in human history."

Esther leaves the Oval Office, pride filling her chest like a balloon. She smiles brightly as she walks past Secretary Geithner, who is now preparing to walk through the same door she is exiting. She knows her day is not over, but all she can think about now is getting home and sharing the news with her family. Years ago, her family escaped war and hardship to come to the United States. Now Esther is about to tell her family that the president of the United States had called her in to thank her for her story—which she knew was really their story.

Esther is never not on call, and she is never alone. When news reached her in the dead of night that ten Peace Corps volunteers were coming under heavy fire in Kyrgyzstan, Esther woke up her daughter at 3:00 A.M. to man the phones while she mobilized her contacts; within hours an Air Force jet was airlifting the volunteers to safety. While she is working at her Peace Corps office, sometimes for eighteen hours a day, her parents watch over the home and the kids with an indefatigable passion. Just like the pictures in her office, her family doesn't simply watch over her—they are the reason she is who she is.

5

....

The Lesson of the Risk Taker

The Gamble of Doing Nothing

When I answered the phone, I was surprised to hear the voice of my friend Alex. He was the director of a major division at an old-school white-shoe investment bank. He looked like something out of an Abercrombie and Fitch catalog, with a tall, athletic frame and classic good looks that suggested days spent on the trading floor and weekends spent at the country club. But while Alex may have seemed like a cookie-cutter scion of privilege, our friendship was real. And I could tell from the tone in his voice that something was wrong.

"Hey, Wes, you have a second to talk?"

"Of course, man. Is everything all right?"

"Not really."

Alex sounded shaken, a rare enough event that I was immediately anxious.

"What happened?"

"They just told me my job is gone."

At first I thought he meant he'd been fired. I was shocked, because Alex was one of the smartest people in finance, and his area of specialty, leveraged buyouts, was one of the hottest areas in all of banking. LBOs, as they're called, are when companies are taken over using money borrowed against the company itself. The practice had fallen out of favor in recent years, the result of lingering scandals from the 1980s and changes in market conditions, but in the last few years we'd entered an era of mega-buyouts, a tide of acquisitions driven by low interest rates and a looser regulatory and lending environment. Those loose standards were starting to cause rumbles of concern on Wall Street and the investment market was starting to turn, but I'd have assumed that someone as competent as Alex would be fine. How could Alex have gotten fired?

I had been sitting in a friend's living room watching football on a Sunday evening when Alex called. Between Alex's shaky voice in one ear and the roar of the NFL in the other, I felt disoriented, like I was between worlds. I stepped into the hallway.

"I am so sorry, man. Did you see this coming?"

"Wes, you don't understand. It's not just my job that's gone. Our *company* is gone. Lehman is liquidating."

That Sunday evening, September 14, 2008, I found out the news that would change the world the next morning. Lehman Brothers, one of the oldest and largest investment banks in the world, was no more.

Lehman started in 1850 as a cotton trading business and quickly grew into a broader commodities trading brokerage, led by brothers Henry and Emanuel Lehman. The brothers had a vision for a growing business, but they probably never could have anticipated the size and scale it would ultimately achieve. By 2008, it was the

fourth-largest pure investment bank in the entire world, trailing
only Goldman Sachs, Morgan Stanley, and Merrill Lynch. It had a
hand in every aspect of the investment banking business and em-
ployed more than twenty-six thousand people, including Alex.

The news wasn't only of academic interest to me, as I was back
on Wall Street by this time. After completing my White House Fellowship, I'd been spun back into a web of uncertainty. I had
amassed a collection of experiences over the past few years, but I
had no true "profession." Many of the friends I'd graduated with
were now on year six of their jobs, deepening their skills and experiences in a specific area of expertise. I felt like a dilettante by com-
parison. It wasn't that I hadn't been busy; I'd been to London and
Afghanistan and Washington, D.C. But my search for what felt
right was starting to make me anxious—I was now preparing to
start my fourth job in almost as many years. There was a voice in
my head that was telling me that it was time for me to get serious,
to focus.

I'd again spent some time thinking about finding my passion.
The experience that had given me the greatest sense of fulfillment
was, unquestionably, my time in the army. The opportunity to lead
soldiers in combat and serve my country in a time of war had
been, in a strange way, one of the great joys of my life. I was now a
senior captain in the Army Reserve, but also recently married. I
saw how difficult the deployment had been on Dawn, the love of
my life, and had no interest in putting any more of that stress on
my young marriage or my wife. So going back on active duty and
continuing to deploy was probably not in the cards for me. In the
absence of passion, I fell back on other motivations. The easiest
choice, I decided, would be to head back to the world of finance. I
had done well at my old firm and already had an offer of a job

should I want to return. I thought more about the idea of actually trying to invest myself in something—to develop expertise in a thing and to feel a sense of completion. I had spent two years in finance, but two years is not enough to claim an understanding of an industry. And, to be honest, part of me wanted to feel not just that I had experienced a lot of interesting and fulfilling things but that I had truly mastered them—for myself and for the people who'd counted on and supported me my whole life. I wasn't in love with banking, but at that moment it didn't matter. I made the trek back to Manhattan and began the interview process at various firms.

Once again, I memorized all the requisite talking points I needed. I dusted off my old finance books and put new batteries in the calculator. I prepared myself as if I were traveling back to a foreign country, with its own laws and language, where knowing the difference between EBITDA (earnings before interest, taxes, debt, and amortization) and net income, or between inherent and intrinsic value, was like knowing the difference between formal and informal verb forms. By the summer, just before I completed my year in Washington, I was set to return to New York and return to finance, this time for Citigroup, working for its Global Technology group. I had no idea that my "safe" choice would soon go through a historic cataclysm.

I went home to Baltimore in early August 2007, preparing for my wife and me to head to New York to begin work. I drove over to Garland Hall at Johns Hopkins University to meet with a mentor, William Brody, who at the time was president of Johns Hopkins. He'd ask me to stop in and give him an update on what I was going to do next in my life. President Brody was not one to suffer fools, nor did he hesitate to voice his opinion if he thought an idea didn't make sense. One of the reasons I ended up choosing Citigroup was because of an introduction from President Brody to Pam Flaherty, who was not only the head of the Citi Foundation but chair of the board at Johns Hopkins. When she heard that I was interested in going back into finance, she made it very clear that Citi was where I needed to go. The entrée into the firm she gave me was invaluable.

When I walked into his office and sat down across from him, President Brody leaned forward. There was a moment of silence.

"So, what are your plans for next?" he asked at last.

I smiled and said, "Well, I think you will be happy to hear that I have decided to return to Wall Street."

He sat back and stared at me for a moment. "Really?"

That hadn't quite been the response I was expecting.

"What is your thinking about why this is the right move?" he asked. But his body language told me that there would be no answer that would really make sense to him.

Even so, I started to explain my need for a sense of completion, my need to be successful, to make some money. As expected, none of these answers seemed to move him.

"Is this, deep in your heart, what you want to do? Or is it something you feel you should do?"

"Probably the latter," I muttered, feeling suddenly exposed.

"Wes, I am going to be very honest," he said, his eyes narrowing. "If you feel the need to go and do something you are not passionate about, for whatever reason, then that is a decision you have to make. But I am going to tell you, the day you feel you have accomplished what you need to accomplish there, leave. Because every day you stay longer than you have to, you become extraordinarily ordinary."

I left the meeting even more uncertain about what I was doing, about what I *should* be doing. But my fellowship was up, I had a life to get on with, and I was running out of time to figure out my next move, so I took the default option. What could be safer than a job on Wall Street, the heart of the American economy?

Days after Alex called me to let me know about his job, I watched as Lehman's collapse sent tidal waves through the finance industry—and from there to the entire American and world economy. While the numbers were shocking—Lehman's $600 billion of debt, AIG bailed out for $85 billion, the Dow losing close to 800 points in one day, the CalPERS pension fund losing over $50 billion, Citi's $306 billion in risky assets taken over by the government—it was the stories of individual lives disrupted that really invaded my psyche. The crash wasn't just devastating for billionaires; people all over the country—all over the world—suffered losses: lost jobs, diminished pensions, houses stripped of value. And more immediately for me, many of my colleagues in the banking world were the collateral victims of the reckless excess that had taken over some areas of finance.

"Today is my last day at the firm" was the opening line in many of the emails I received over those weeks. I sat at my desk and watched as a parade of coworkers made the dreaded march into the boss's office, accompanied by the reluctant executioners of the human resources department, and walk out with a handshake and instructions about how to wrap up their employment and leave the building. The hallways on trading floors were now crowded with cardboard boxes filled to the top with "tombstones"—notebooks of successfully executed deals—and framed pictures of family members, the same family members most bankers openly acknowledged not having spent enough time with over the years. These people hadn't just lost a job; they'd lost an identity. They'd spent countless hours demonstrating loyalty to the business, knowing, of course, that they were only as valuable as their last deal. But this is the trick that a job can sometimes play on us: we know we're working at the pleasure of a manager, an owner, a corporation, but we're human and can't help but develop emotional attachments to the work we do. We begin to identify ourselves with our employers and believe that a business can return our loyalty. Sometimes businesses do. But when it comes down to it, a corporation's first allegiance is to its own survival. Everyone benefits from the idea that we're all in it together—until suddenly we're not.

I know it's hard to feel sympathy for bankers, especially at a moment when the banking system had so distorted the world's economy. But when you're in close proximity to the people affected, you also see it as a series of specific, human tragedies. And it wasn't only bankers I was saying goodbye to on a seemingly daily basis. There were also people like Ramón.

I met Ramón my very first week at Citi. For everyone in our department, dinner was a burger or salad ordered in and eaten at our desks. Soon after I started at Citi, I realized that, as had been the case at Deutsche Bank in London, all three meals were going to be eaten with my colleagues, talking about deals, pop culture, bosses, or our pathetic social lives.

On this night I sat at my desk, looking through a spreadsheet I was having difficulty comprehending, the ranks of numbers and formulas marching in dizzying circles. Half-empty containers of Chinese food huddled next to me, the remnants of egg foo yung doused with duck sauce and hot mustard adding a disturbingly organic smell to the recycled office air.

"Hello, sir!" said a cheery voice that momentarily took me away from the row of numbers in front of me.

"Hey," I replied, and returned my gaze to the screen. I was not-so-inadvertently giving the impression of not wanting to be bothered. I didn't want to be rude, but I also didn't want to talk. I wanted to finish my work so I could go home.

Ramón reached under my desk and pulled out my industrial gray trash can, filled with papers, water bottles, and bits of fried rice. "I haven't seen you around, are you new?" he asked. I knew that I stuck out at my job, on my floor. And it wasn't because of my height or grease-stained shirt. It was because the Technology Group at Citi was not a place known for African American bankers.

"Yeah, just got here a week ago," I replied flatly, staring more intently at my screen.

Ramón took the clear plastic bag out of my trash can and replaced it with a new one, taking my leftovers with him.

"OK. Well, I really proud to see you here, Mr. Moore."

Maybe it was the way he said it, with his broken English and strong accent. Maybe it was his voice, deep, sturdy, aged. He sounded like so many members of my own family. But I didn't know what he looked like, because in that moment I didn't even have the decency, or curiosity, to pick my head up.

With a sigh I put the spreadsheet down, figuring it wasn't going anywhere, and looked up. Handsome but worn, Ramón appeared to be in his early sixties, although I found out later he was in his early fifties. His salt-and-pepper mustache curled as he smiled.

"Please, call me Wes."

I felt awkward that a man so much my senior was calling me "Mr." anything. He knew my name because of the gold-colored name tag that sat outside my office space. I knew his name because of the "Ramón" stitched in black on his tan uniform.

"OK, Mr. Wes."

I smiled. He walked off to the next cubicle and continued to collect trash. I heard a distant "Hello, Mr. Shah" as my eyes drifted back to my spreadsheet.

This was the ritual for a few more days before Ramón and I finally struck up a real conversation. I learned that he was from the Dominican Republic and had come to the United States fifteen years earlier. He had been an accountant in his native country, but the money he was making there was not enough to give him the life he wanted for himself, let alone for the two kids he and his wife shared. One of their children was grown and living in the Dominican Republic. The other was a senior in high school in the Bronx, where Ramón lived, and preparing for college. He was so proud of her; he carried her picture in his wallet.

Monday through Friday, between seven and eight in the evening, I came to look forward to my brief conversations with Ramón and his infectious smile. I asked him the secret to a good marriage. We discussed our mutually beloved New York Mets. We talked about his hope to save up some money so he could see his son and his grandchildren in the Dominican Republic. He was a trained accountant who was now picking up the trash of a twenty-eight-year-old because doing so provided a better life for his family. He had decades more work experience in the field than I did. He had probably forgotten more about accounting than I had learned at that point. All things being equal, there should have been a way for him to be sitting at the desk next to me, to take what he knew about numbers and the world and translate it into analytics that would shape our country's financial future. But we are still very much a country where accidents of birth and arbitrary opportunities can still accelerate or encumber an individual's chances for success. Although I didn't know it at the time, despite my challenges, even I had been a beneficiary of birth and opportunity, on the inside track to a path of opportunities that simply didn't exist for Ramón.

After the financial collapse, and during the period when those of us lucky enough to still have jobs were deluged by emails from those who no longer did, I was stricken with feelings of anxiety, sadness, and maybe some survivor's guilt. The people who had been let go weren't all silver-spoon legacies; most of them were people who had worked hard, done what they were asked to do, studied at the right schools, and taken on huge amounts of debt to educate themselves and make everyone around them proud. The people I knew were not management—I wasn't getting emails from Dick Fuld or Jimmy Cayne. My friends at the junior level were not responsible for the crisis. They were not the ones who made the rules or, in the vast majority of cases, even worked in the divisions that caused the damage. But it didn't matter. I felt terrible as I watched so many walk through the doors carrying those cardboard boxes. But none hit me harder than seeing Ramón that November night.

I was walking to the restroom around 5:00 P.M., just as the sun was setting for the evening, when I saw Ramón standing at the elevator bank.

"Hey, Ramón!" I called out. I wasn't expecting to see him so early.

"Hi, Mr. Wes," he answered.

He was not as cheery as I was used to seeing him. I asked him what was going on, and he told me that he had just been informed that he no longer had a job.

"Everybody gone," he said, a look of confusion on his face. It was an unsettling reminder of that first conversation I'd had with Alex all those months ago.

"You mean the entire team was let go?" I asked. I was almost afraid to know the answer.

"Yes, sir."

I didn't know what to say. The standard lines that I used for my other colleagues didn't quite apply: *Someone on the Street will pick you up.* Or *With your skill set, another firm is going to scoop you right up.* Or *Just tap into your university network.* Or *Don't worry, take some time, you have a while before you have to make a decision about next steps.* It wasn't true that all of my former colleagues on Wall Street would find another place in the industry, but they all had the education and the connections necessary to weather the storms of reinvention. I knew from our conversations, though, that Ramón's salary in maintenance did double duty: supporting his family in New York and making life easier for his family back in the Dominican Republic. At the end of his night shift, Ramón had precious little energy or money left to fund a new dream or make a plan for the future.

"Ramón, I am so sorry," I said, and meant it.

"Thank you, sir. It's OK. I have to tell my family, and it will be fine. Don't worry."

We shook hands and exchanged goodbyes. I stood and watched as Ramón entered the elevator. As the doors closed, I waved goodbye once more. Walking back to my desk, imagining the conversation Ramón was going to have with his family later that night, I said a prayer for him and a prayer of gratitude for myself. Tonight was not the night that I would have to go home and tell my wife that I no longer had a job.

Close to thirty thousand people on Wall Street lost their jobs during the financial crisis. With all the uncertainty around us, the rest of us simply put our heads down and worked. *No need for stressing or worrying out loud,* we told each other. *Remember your blessings. Keep working hard.*

My work was complicated by a passion project I had been working on in secret. For the past year I had been writing a book about a young man I'd come to know—a man who woke up to a very different daily reality than mine, but with whom I shared a number of other similarities, including our names. I would wake up at five-thirty every morning, write for two hours about the other Wes Moore, and then head to the office. On some mornings words would spill out of me almost uncontrollably—emotions, memories, and ideas flowing through my heart and mind and onto the screen. Other mornings I would stare at a blinking cursor, watching as it appeared and disappeared from my screen like a hypnotist's trick.

The story I was writing was about a man named Wes Moore who, just as I was receiving my Rhodes Scholarship years ago, was being sentenced to life in prison for the murder of a police officer in Baltimore. I initially learned about him when my mother told me—half in shock—that there were wanted posters with my name on them in my neighborhood in Baltimore. I followed his case as it developed, not just because it was a dramatic and tragic tale of

murder but because in some strange way I felt somehow impli-
cated in it. After more exploration, I realized how much Wes and I
had in common aside from our names. We lived in the same city,
both grew up in single-parent households, and were around the
same age. In childhood we'd had similar experiences with depriva-
tion of resources, with law enforcement, with school. One day I
just decided to reach out to him. I wasn't sure if he would write
back. He was, after all, in prison for life, with no possibility of pa-
role for his unforgiving decision. But I had questions I wanted to
ask, and Wes was the only one who could answer them. So one day
I sent him a letter.

To my surprise, about a month later a letter came back to me
from Jessup Correctional Institution in Maryland with answers.
But his response only triggered more questions. The one letter
turned into dozens. Those dozens of letters turned into dozens of
visits. Years later, I started to write about it.

By 2008, after the crisis hit, I was spending part of each workday
bracing myself for alarming job reports and discouraging market
numbers. Every time I saw the horrible detritus of the crisis—as
when one of my greatest friends and role models came to me to
borrow some money to pay his light bill, because the home he was
living in, with its underwater mortgage and foreclosure proceed-
ings in process, was pitch dark—I thought about how unfair it all
was. Why did we have to go through this? But then I would start
the next day the same way I'd started the last, by reading letters
from someone who is assured of spending the rest of his life in jail,
or reading articles about a police officer, a father of five, who went
to work one day and never came home. For me, at least, beginning
my mornings that way wrapped the rest of the day's struggles in
some perspective.

My panic and sense of injustice faded. It wasn't just about the subjects of my book; it was a reminder that for all the turmoil on Wall Street, there were people out there who had it much worse than I did, living with burdens I wouldn't wish on anyone. The officer stolen from his family. The family of the other Wes, who now suffer because of his decisions. Ramón. The kids in hurricane-ravaged Mississippi still living in trailers. My friends in Afghanistan, both American soldiers and Afghans like Abdullah. The kids I grew up with in Baltimore and the Bronx. Instead of thinking about the relative decline of a group of people who could still count themselves among the luckiest in the history of the planet—or, even more appalling, thinking about my own predicament despite my tremendous good fortune—I started to think once again about what contribution I was making to the real struggles I'd already lived through and seen for myself, up close, close enough to touch and never forget.

Months later, after the book was released, the economy and many of our lives had still not settled down. In the case of the economy, we hadn't even seen the bottom of the market collapse yet. My job description had changed in a telling way. Where previously I'd focused exclusively on investments and ways to find interesting returns, I was now working on divestiture, or ways to get things off our company balance sheets. I still worked hard and was still being paid. I'd survived the worst of the industry's contraction, and it was clear that finance, of all industries, would rebound from the crisis. But one thing was becoming increasingly clear to me: I no longer wanted to be there.

I didn't regret my decision to return to finance. I met some remarkable people and honed a set of skills. To some degree, I felt a sense of completion. But now I was realizing that staying somewhere for a long time doesn't make the place home. Banking wasn't home, so why anchor myself there as if it was? I thought back on President Brody's comments: *extraordinarily ordinary.* I knew why I had come to Wall Street, but it was time to go.

This time, though, change would not come in the form of a mentor's advice or the well-timed arrival of a fellowship or educational opportunity. I needed to go home and powwow with the woman who was the VIP of my game-of-life team. I needed to talk to my partner.

On my way home that day, the train car I was in was eerily quiet despite the late hour. In the car with me were a couple, eyes closed, her head snuggled against his shoulder, and an older man, his tweed jacket a size too small for him, huddled forward with an intense stare. I sighed deeply and placed my headphones into my ears. My music player shuffled to a song I hadn't heard in a while but whose words were remarkably apt.

The song opens up with a scratchy allusion to old vinyl records, full of pops and clicks. Quickly a flowing piano introduction interrupts, and seconds later Lauryn Hill's striking voice enters, as if to tell the music behind her to wait. The power behind her voice is captivating, but on that evening her words were unsettling. My eyes closed. I knew this song. I knew where she was going. But I listened as if it were the first time.

The song is about how life can sometimes squeeze you so tight you can't breathe. But then the song's chorus reveals the answer to her dilemma:

But deep in my heart, the answer it was in me
And I made up my mind to define my own destiny.

She draws out the word "deeeep," stressing how she knows the answer's there even though it might be hard to see at first. That *deeeep* means *keep digging*.

We were having a conversation. Or maybe a therapy session. When the song ended, I put it on repeat and listened to Lauryn talk to me—speak to me—for the rest of the ride home.

My stop arrived, and the older man stood up and walked off the train before me. The couple stayed on the train, sleeping. Lauryn and I headed home.

When I got there, my wife was getting ready for bed. We always talked about our days when I got in, about the high points and about the frustrations. Best moments and worst moments—it was a ritual we shared each evening, regardless of what time I managed to come in.

"Best moment?" she asked me.

I told her about my conversation with Lauryn. Then I told her that in spite of everything I enjoyed about my work—and the security it gave us—I was deeply unhappy. We sat together in bed, my rumpled suit still on, my tie now loosened around my opened collar, and I decided to just unload everything that had been on my mind for these past months—the anxiety and the sudden clarity that I was in the wrong place, doing the wrong work. Finally at some point I stopped talking and looked at her. She was just sitting there smiling.

"What? What's so funny? What do you think?"

"I think you already know the answer."

She was right. I knew there were real risks to leaving a steady job, a consistent salary, benefits, health care, retirement account—all the things we needed and relied on. Leaving that can be nerve-racking, particularly when you know there are other people relying on you. I looked at her again, and she said four words that helped alleviate all of my worry and uncertainty.

"I believe in you."

"I believe in us," I responded.

I wasn't sure what the next steps were going to be, but I was fine with that. I just knew that I needed to make a change, and that night my partner gave me the confidence to take my dreams out of the box I'd locked them in and trust that there would be enough security in my journey to carry us through. We had very real responsibilities, including a mortgage that was due regardless of what I told the bank about "following my passion," a need for health insurance to cover me and my family, aging parents, a desire for children. There's always a reason not to make a change; it's rare that everything perfectly aligns and we can announce to ourselves that now is the right time to change everything. But while time moves on, our feelings of unhappiness or aimlessness tend to stubbornly stick around.

The next morning, I didn't hit the snooze button or wonder how it could be that another day was about to begin when the last one had just ended. A sense of peace replaced the confusion that had filled my stomach hours before. I gulped down my morning tea. I began to make a list of the people whom I had to tell that I was quitting, the mentors and friends who had been supportive of me for years. I thought about Pam Flaherty, the head of the board of trustees at Johns Hopkins and the head of the Citigroup Foundation, who had helped me land the job at Citi in the first place. I thought about my boss, Ray McGuire, who had become more like a father figure. He was not only one of the top African Americans in finance but also one of the best, most interesting people of any race in finance. "Main Man, relish the details of the business," he would tell me in his boisterous baritone. The nickname "Main Man" always meant a lot to me, because, unbeknownst to him, that was the name my father had called me before he died. Ray's shadow loomed large, and I'd become not simply a better banker but a better person because of him. I thought about my colleagues and friends: Christina and Julie, Sandy and Vishal, Mustafa and Josh. People I had spent hours upon hours with, shared three meals a day with, people who I saw more than my own family.

On the walk to the train station that morning, I called up my friend Reggie, who worked for a rival firm. I told him that I was going to resign and go out on my own.

"Wow, man, you sure about this?" he asked.

"I am. I feel good about it."

We were still in the middle of "the great layoff," where entire groups and divisions were losing jobs. Employers were well past cutting out the fat and were now digging deep into muscle and bone to reduce expenses. Reggie was concerned I would not be able to find a new job. His concern was real because he knew my responsibilities were real. All I knew for sure about my next move was that I would find work that was entrepreneurial, that tried to solve a real problem in the real world, and that was service-focused. Something that felt like it mattered. Something I loved.

"It's just so risky," he said worriedly. "I really think you should reconsider."

I told him that the riskiest thing would be for me to stay in a place where I didn't feel like I was growing. There was never any guarantee that things would be successful, whether you are doing something you love or something you dislike. Life is full of challenges and risks. Nothing is guaranteed, ever. I knew that. But I wanted to pursue something that I was excited about, whatever that was.

"I wish you luck, man."

"Thanks, Reg. I appreciate that."

Six months later I received a call from Reggie letting me know that he'd just been laid off from his firm after working there for six years. He was on his way home to explain to his wife and three children.

Reggie, of course, had no way of telling what the future held. But if I had made the decision he'd counseled me to make, I know it would've just been out of fear. I would've let fear of not being hired again by another bank stop me from doing what I wanted with my life.

I began to recognize that the best decisions I had made in my life were the ones where I let go of fear and had confidence in myself, my training, and God. Ironically, each success fostered a momentary amnesia about its foundation. I found myself in a complicated place where the more "successful" I became, the more I clung to "safety," almost as if I'd completely forgotten most of the tenets that had made me successful in the first place.

One Rhodes Scholar who became a dear friend (and, along with his wife, Marcy, godparents to our son) is John Macbain, an entrepreneur and philanthropist. He would joke with me about how sometimes the people with the most promise are also the most fearful, and in many cases fear is what keeps that promise from turning into action. John doesn't look the part of the corporate hero—he's not the tall, silver-tongued all-American boy. Instead, he's wired for productive impatience. His hustle, hard work, and focus are what created his success.

There was a book that was published a generation ago—*Fear of Falling* by Barbara Ehrenreich. She talked about the fear that middle-class people lived with, fear that they'd lose their jobs, fear that they'd fall all the way to the bottom. That fear created conformity, spurred conservatism, and stifled creative thinking; in fact, it stifled lives and killed dreams. We're at a moment now where many of the fears that paralyzed previous generations have actually come to pass. We live in a time of uncertainty about our own security, a time of uncertainty about the economy. But the good thing about having your fears realized—as happened when I watched Wall Street collapse over a matter of months—is that it also eliminates those fears. There's nothing to be afraid of anymore, so we can own our lives again.

This massive, unsettling insecurity is also a license to infuse our professional aspirations with our soul's calling, to dig deep and listen to what thrills us as well as what we think might pay the bills. When we have nothing to lose, when we realize that nothing is certain, we are freer than ever to choose our own path.

THE WORKER #5

■ ■ ■ ■ ■ ■ ■ ■ ■ ■ ■ ■ ■ ■ ■ ■ ■ ■ ■

The Risk Taker

CARA ALEY
Co-founder, American Mojo

"I can accept failure. Everyone fails at something. I can't accept not trying."

Cara Aley, tall and striking, leans forward as she quotes Michael Jordan's words. Her smile, easy and disarming, flashes as she speaks. The story of the company Cara cofounded with her brothers, American Mojo, is a story about belief, effort, risk, success—and failure. When we're looking for our work in life, there's no question that sometimes we'll fail. But failure looks different when it happens as part of a larger life plan. Then it can look like just another step on the path, however difficult a step it may be.

D arr, Tom, and Cara Aley are a Norman Rockwell–esque triad of strapping, good-natured, whip-smart siblings, twin brothers who are forty-seven years old and their sister, younger by eleven years. They dug into a late-morning meal at a Manhattan hotel for deal-making hipsters, infecting each other with the buoyant optimism of bred-in-the-bone entrepreneurs on a mission to save at least part of the world. With American Mojo, they plan to raise single mothers up out of poverty, pay them living wages in sustainable jobs, surround them with 360 degrees of support (health care, quality child care, English as a Second Language classes, GED preparation, home budget literacy, counseling), and offer career-advancement skills development and opportunities. After two years of intense conversation about strategy and execution, the Aleys launched their for-profit social venture, American Mojo, in 2010. They'd sussed out the possibilities and settled on apparel manufacturing, with a factory in Lowell, Massachusetts, which was the birthplace of the Industrial Revolution and the crucible of the domestic textile industry.

It was a carefully thought-out if exhilaratingly chancy enterprise, especially since none of them had experience in anything even remotely related. But the Aley men have twenty-five wildly successful years of new business expertise between them, and Cara brought her own entrepreneurial drive to the Mojo party.

The three cooked up a knockout business plan. The Aley twins put in start-up and operating capital from their own reservoirs, along with the finely honed strategic know-how of successful serial entrepreneurs. Cara put the pedal to the metal on operations, from hiring and the shop floor to website management and developing the signature employee assistance program. They covered all the angles to get them to the point where outside investors with a dedication to the social good would step up and fuel growth.

The idea was simple. As a tribute to their own single mother, they would create a business that would support other single mothers. The company name, American Mojo, stands for "American Mothers and Jobs." The people they would hire, from the top executives to the lowest employees, would be single mothers, many of whom were living in poverty.

"It was Tom's idea," Cara explains. "He was running a mitten drive at a church, and we all knew that wasn't a permanent solution. He knew we had to provide jobs for the parents of the kids getting the mittens if we were going to ever change things."

Two years after the 2010 launch, the family was on a high. They had revenues of about $3 million, much of it from big clients like Zazzle, a West Coast custom manufacturer and online retailer. They were carefully scaling up operations and expected to reach profitability. They were learning fast how to smooth out production cycles, about navigating price volatility, and how to cope with the iffy dependability of overseas suppliers.

"We had a tough experience with a Chinese supplier," says Cara. "They sent six thousand yards of fabric with giant holes and dirt streaks. It had a 15 percent shrinkage rate. That was it. Now I'm negotiating with an American supplier. They're great."

Staunch made-in-America advocates, believers in bringing back industry from overseas and creating sustainable jobs, they scouted out sources that fit their ideological bill. "If you actually act decently, you could put programs in place that would give people wages they could live on," Cara says. "Made in the USA is an obvious way to tackle unemployment, and more and more customers are seeking out that label."

"It's amazing how many people and companies say they want to help but don't lend a hand because, at the end of the day, cost is king," Darr continues. "We talked to the top thirty U.S. brands. Each one has corporate responsibility goals, but it takes an enormous amount of time to get them to do anything of meaning. We've had to change our business plan to higher-margin products. Social mission gets you in the door, but you better have an economic plan or they won't be able to get behind it."

American Mojo found a niche for itself in custom manufacturing, also known as "me commerce"—that is, giving a customer a way to make a product uniquely his/her own. Products range from shoes (Nike has cleaned up on sneakers) to dish towels, cups, mugs, blankets—you name it. And people will pay up to 50 percent more for products with their own stamp. "Customization is a space that American manufacturers can justify because the market is there," explains Darr.

The trajectory of the Aley family set the tone for the American Mojo story. Aside from Darr, Tom, and Cara, there are two other siblings: an older sister, Dana, and a younger brother, Doug.

Their father left the family for "the love of his life," a woman he'd known in college, when Cara was five and Doug was two and a half. Tom and Darr were sixteen-year-old high school sophomores, and Dana was eighteen. "I knew nothing about it," says Cara of the fraying of their parents' relationship. "They were very good, I never saw them arguing. They had a nice friendship, but they weren't in love."

A dedicated dad, their father "never missed a child support payment and paid for college," Cara says. "Dad is an entrepreneur himself, and it's because of him that we have this spirit and drive that we do. We all worked in Dad's business in summer internships."

Things were harder for her mother, an elementary school librarian with a master's degree; the divorce left her bitter. "My mom struggled on her own," recalls Cara. "She was sad and this was tough. She never sought therapy and never wanted to meet anyone else. Doug and I, especially, saw the pain.

"She was this person of such incredible strength. She'd advocate for us, coming to school and demanding the teacher drive the curriculum to make sure we got the best education. She made sure that even though we were in a small town we'd get the right thing. She found strength for her kids. And that was a total inspiration."

Trying to climb her way out of financial straits, the Aley matriarch tried her hand at entrepreneurial pursuits, but "she wouldn't accept Dad's help. She was very independent." She took a stab at real estate and tried her hand as a research consultant, though neither succeeded. But she brought technology to her school, built her own website, and digitized the school library.

The relationship between Cara and her mom grew fraught over the years, and when she was thirteen, Cara moved in with her father and his wife because she felt like she was living in an "unhealthy environment." It set a pattern. "When something didn't feel like a good decision or a comfortable place for me to be, I left it—whether it was a relationship or a job. Life's too short to waste it on being unhappy. Only you can change your situation. Complaining about it is a waste of time."

But the separation took a big toll on the mother-daughter relationship. "I think I saw how much it hurt her when I left. And how your mother, who's always been your role model, has been reduced to tears because of a decision you made. To see at thirteen that you can have such an impact on someone's happiness was heavy."

For a year after, tension ran high and letters flew back and forth as her mother tried to figure out why Cara left. Over time, the anger and the angst subsided. The siblings credit their mother with fostering a sense of closeness among them that is unshakable.

"My older siblings have been my rock. Such a positive influence. I just feel that net. We have all the good things and the challenging things that we share among us," says Cara.

It is also the fabric that lines everything that American Mojo set out to do. As they built the business, the siblings felt a strong sense of responsibility toward the people who worked for them.

"If things go awry, it's a lot of people whose lives are impacted. Inefficiencies have a negative impact. If we have an order to get out fast and expedite, it has a ripple effect. We wanted this to be a place of stability and positivity, not stress. I mean, a certain amount of stress is healthy and inevitable. But it weighed on me," Cara says.

In the summer of 2012, Cara was bringing GED and ESL classes on-site. She brought in Budget Buddies, a one-on-one mentoring program to help employees create household budgets for themselves. There was a matching retirement plan, but Mojo management was working with a nonprofit to determine if matching savings accounts made more sense. There was the possibility of free college educations for employees' offspring through Endicott College. Employees got assistance with everything from finding nutritional foods for their families on a budget to accessing benefits such as food stamps.

"We want to help them have the best chance to have a better life for themselves and their kids," Cara explains. "We're taking a two-generation approach." She cites studies showing that quality early-childhood education significantly lowers high school dropout rates.

"We want to break the cycle of poverty. This is where it starts."

They were all plagued by a sense of urgency. "The level of detail orientation on the business side alone is overwhelming," said Cara. "Everything that can go wrong will. And the little things that go wrong have a ripple effect." That fabric from China? In addition to its defects, it came two months late. "We lost five months of manufacturing time. We were lucky to have a patient customer."

By 2012, Mojo was launching the biggest customization project, a jacket with ten to fifteen parts, eight colors for the shell, four different materials, zippers in different colors. It involved a massive amount of setup and complex inventory management.

They'd launched a program called Momtrepreneurs, providing employees with a chance to execute their own designs for distribution on the Mojo website, earning a commission.

The possibilities and the reality left Tom teary. His favorite story, and one that symbolizes so many others, involves a staffer he calls C.D., who designed a little wool wallet that sold online for about $20, providing a profit of about 30 percent. "I sold it through the college market en masse—three hundred schools. C.D. comes with an eight-year-old boy to collect her checks. One was payroll and the other was commission, and it was a big check." In the middle of the story, Tom chokes up again. "Her son high-fives her. That's the high point for me. The problems with welfare is it becomes self-perpetuating and institutionalized because kids are watching what their parents do. Well, C.D. started crying. The son and I high-fived it. And I said, 'Here you're on three hundred different college campuses.' Her son could see that she had created something. That's where the cycle is broken. What matters is sustainability. It's to break the institutionalization of poverty. We break it one mom at a time."

They were so close to credible, big-time success—but then things caved in.

The company was poised to soar. A deal to acquire American Mojo, underwritten by a for-profit company and a foundation, was on the fast track, and the cash infusion from the deal would have freed the siblings to run the business exactly as they planned. After a year of chasing down funding, racing from one potential investor to the next, this was the big payoff. Cara was in the throes of managing Mojo's West Coast expansion, nailing down a manufacturing facility, securing anchor tenants and clients.

But in early September, the acquisition collapsed, burying American Mojo and the dream. The Calvert Foundation, a social impact private equity fund, was ready to put half a million dollars into the Aleys' vision but demanded a co-investor to add capital and be the responsible party on the board. Enter JP Selects, a global online shipping portal for eco-conscious brands, part of the Paul Mitchell hair-products empire. However, Calvert made a last-minute discovery that JP Selects was developing an upscale brand of spirits, and Calvert's guidelines prohibit consorting with purveyors of alcohol. Mojo, devoted to hoodies, T-shirts, fleece blankets, housewares, totes, and other such products, got caught in the crossfire.

Within days, Cara had to break the news to the company's employees that they would be closing in four weeks. In those remaining weeks Mojo staff filled orders while Cara and management staff scurried to wind down operations, with the highest priority given to helping their mostly single-mom staff of unskilled workers find other jobs.

"I'm thoroughly exhausted from trying so hard to raise money, and manufacturing is a grind. I'm a bit burned out from so much work on the ground," says Cara. "There were high highs and low lows. That's emotionally exhausting. When you get body-slammed time after time, when you get a big order and for one reason or another it doesn't work out . . . it gets to be too much."

The failure was heartbreaking to the family, because this was not simply another business. "I'm dismayed and upset," confesses Darr. "We believe we had a tremendous opportunity and enough time to build relationships with big brands to make a meaningful impact. To see it fall apart was extremely sad. I'm much more upset emotionally than financially. If I had to do it all over again, I would. But we'd start to look for financial partners first. All the eleven or twelve companies Tom and I started before American Mojo, we didn't do that. We built the businesses first and then looked for partners. That way we could retain more of the business and keep control. Our biggest weakness is we didn't know anything about this sector. We had to learn quick. We are all proud of our accomplishments but felt we could achieve more. It was about sustainability, building a company that could help underserved women. We helped for two years. We were able to help a small population. The thing is, we didn't want to create a lemonade stand, we wanted to be Tropicana."

The social investing sector is growing, but there are still challenges. "For-profit is a small part of that," said Darr. "The access to capital is hard to find. We talked to two hundred people and organizations—foundations, billionaires, venture capitalists, and wealthy individuals. There was a "No" behind every door. I don't think their hearts could believe in sustainable manufacturing in this country. If we'd been able to get enough money to sustain Mojo for another year, history would have led to those investors being more aggressive."

He believes that there's a huge opportunity to marry the for-profit model with doing social good—think the shoe company Tom's. But for the Aleys, there's another factor: it's not about job creation, it's about kids. When it comes to creating sustainable American jobs, "you have to sharpen the pencil and identify exactly how you're going to do that."

The Aleys may be down, but only for the moment. Cara is beginning to work with Two Degrees, a food bar company that donates a meal to children in need around the world for every two nutrition bars purchased. Darr and Tom are running Rapidbuyr .com, planning to grow it and then exit with rebuilt resources. At the same time they're looking for their next family social venture. Darr imagines that their next opportunity "could very well be tapping into rural communities where poverty is growing faster than in urban ones. Mega call centers where English can't be a second language. If we could create a big office, people could take airline reservations or service calls. Consumers want to talk to someone closer to home than India. Big companies might appreciate that. We could go out and talk to a Dell, an HP, or an American Airlines and convince them it's a social good as well as a sound business move."

Cara is thinking about how to take the wraparound employee

assistance program that was so effective at Mojo to companies like McDonald's, where the labor force remains largely unskilled and the attrition rate is high.

"From a personal growth standpoint, this job has changed my life. I never thought I could run a company before," she says. "I'm a totally different person. My focus has changed and I want to do more social impact work. I'd never done a financial model or pitched a client. Who gets to go from being a director of product development at a technology company to president and COO of a social venture? This has been a huge opportunity. For quite a few years I'd been interested in doing something meaningful with my day, something more fulfilling. I didn't feel any personal satisfaction in my technology bubble except for getting promoted.

"What's interesting was before I stepped into this domain, it was so easy not to see poverty and the pain people are facing every day. When you have a six-figure salary and you drive to work, it's easy to ignore people sleeping under the bridge, to just not see it. Stepping into this world raised my awareness of how difficult so many people have it in this country. And, more important, that we can actually do something about it."

6

■ ■ ■ ■ ■ ■ ■ ■ ■ ■

The Lesson of the Worker

Granting Yourself Permission

"At events like this, many people are tempted to make predictions. At my graduation from Riverdale in 1980, I predicted I would hardly ever see this campus again. I was so remarkably wrong, so remarkably young, and so full of hubristic certainty. Here's another Riverdale-related prediction, this one made twenty years ago by a former Riverdale senior administrator about our speaker today, Wes Moore. Wes was twelve years old then, and this administrator made the following prediction: 'Wes Moore, you will never amount to very much of anything.'"

David Roberts was the chairman of the board of trustees at Riverdale Country School, an elite private school in New York City. Riverdale's campus, nestled along the Hudson River, is impressively intimidating for a K–12 school. Its alumni rolls include some of the top leaders, tastemakers, and trendsetters in government, finance, the arts, and culture. David Roberts, one of the most generous people I've ever known, was one of them. He not only was the proud father of one of the graduates that day but also had the dubious distinction of introducing the graduation speaker that day: me.

I had been nervous about this speech for a long time. Part of it was because I had seen many graduation speakers at many schools before, and the only thing I remember about most of them is that they spoke for far too long. But it was not just the *what* that fueled my apprehension and caution, it was the *where*. As David had alluded, my history with the school was not one that either of us had reason to be proud of.

Close to two decades earlier I had entered Riverdale's campus as a young elementary school student. Riverdale and schools like it fill different roles, depending on the student. Riverdale is, by some estimates, the most expensive, difficult-to-get-into school in the entire country. It brings kids into a world of prestige and high expectations. For some of these kids, this is nothing new: prestige and expectation were their birthright. For others, it was an acknowledgment of early achievements and great potential. And for a few of us who entered, it was neither. For us, Riverdale represented the enormous sacrifice and investment—and hope—of the people who loved us. Even with financial aid, my mother and grandparents had to sacrifice their own financial security so that I could go to Riverdale. My mother sacrificed her present: money she could've used to make her day-to-day life easier. My grandparents sacrificed their past: money they had saved up and equity they had accrued. And all three of them did it because they thought my future was worth it. It was a leap of faith—I'd call it extraordinary, except that I've seen parents all over the world do the same for their kids. And I know I'd do the same for my children now. And maybe that's what makes it so extraordinary—the commonality of that faith in the future, manifested by parents but, really, in a functional society, by all of that society's adults on behalf of all of its children.

I didn't give it much thought back then, but I've had a lot of time to think about it since. Without even the slightest acknowledgment, appreciation, or request for gratitude, my mother worked three different jobs during my time at the school. As my sister used to eloquently put it, "Our mother wore sweaters so we could wear coats." In return for her abundant sacrifice, I selfishly did my best to make sure I left Riverdale under the worst possible terms.

I decided to pick and choose which days I'd go to school. I decided that being the class clown was the best approach to my studies. And I spent a lot of time hurting people who loved me just so I could impress people who didn't even care about me. The greatest "impact" I made on the school was setting a class record for suspensions. I was a legend on campus for all the worst reasons. For instance, there was the day the fire department had to be called in because of a prank involving smoke bombs that I found too irresistible to deny myself. By the time I was in eighth grade, despite the sacrifices of my mom, other family members, and even many people at Riverdale, I had to leave the school.

So when the invitation to be a commencement speaker arrived, I wasn't sure what to say. I was officially asked by the headmaster, Dominic Randolph, a stylish British iconoclast with a sharp sense of humor and an intense passion for building the character of his students as much as for raising their SAT scores.

"Wes Moore!" he chirped into the phone. "I would like to formally invite you to be the commencement speaker for Riverdale's 2012 graduation." When I didn't answer, he said, "Are you there?"

"Yes, sorry," I managed. "I'm still here."

I was trying to think of the most thoughtful, politically correct way of saying no, but nothing came to me. That's when I realized I actually wanted to come back.

"You do know about my academic history at that place, don't you?" I asked.

I heard a chuckle on the other end of the phone.

"We do. Not exactly stellar, I admit, but that is why we are asking you. Most of the damage you have done on campus is just about repaired, so we figured it was time you came back."

"Well, as long as security lets me back on campus, I would love to."

Coming back for graduation was one of the first times I had returned to the school since leaving. I walked around campus thinking about what a wasted opportunity it had been for me. Now I had a better understanding of just how hurtful it was to others when my impulses conquered my better judgment. My mother and grandmother were with me that day on campus, and before I said anything else, I apologized to them. When I left Riverdale I'd been young and naive, and I'd felt alone. It had been a difficult time in my life. My father had died. My family had been uprooted from our home in Maryland and had come to the South Bronx to live with my grandparents just as the plague of crack cocaine was laying waste to the neighborhood. I'd felt alienated from everything and struggled to find a place in the world that felt right, struggled to find an identity that fit; failing that, I acted out. Later in life, I'd find the words that fit my attitude back then in the great Paul Laurence Dunbar poem "We Wear the Mask":

We wear the mask that grins and lies
It hides our teeth and it shades our eyes
This debt we pay for human guile
With torn and bleeding hearts, we smile.

I'd worn the mask daily while I attended Riverdale. I'd wanted something that was probably too complicated to achieve: at the same time I wanted to be recognized, acknowledged—*seen, loved*—I also wanted to go unnoticed and to be left alone. Now, walking that campus as an adult, I felt that odd combination of emotions flooding me again. It was strange to be invited back to a place that I'd last seen from behind a closed gate barring my re-entry. For a long while I had put much of that time in my life behind me; I rarely thought about it because I was embarrassed by the person I used to be. Coming back to the campus helped me get over that; it helped me understand and sympathize with that kid. I was happy to be back, and grateful again for the second chances my life has afforded me . . . although I was still a little embarrassed about the need for them.

With torn and bleeding hearts, we smile.

As David, the head of the board of trustees, completed his introduction, he said, "You know, I'm kind of unhappy not to be able to introduce my friend as a graduate of Riverdale. Dominic and Wes, please come up here."

With a wide grin, he reached under the podium and pulled out a degree from Riverdale Country School, making me an honorary member of the class of 2012. I was shocked and touched. From the audience, my mother beamed powerfully enough to brighten that overcast June morning. She had worked so hard for me to be here, and I was finally able to hold up my end of the bargain. I held the diploma up—it was for her.

As I spoke to the graduates I told them a little bit about some of the dilemmas I've recounted in this book—about the impossibility of knowing what you want to do with your life as soon as you leave campus. We are expected to have an answer to the question "What do you want to be?" but I would argue that most people at that stage don't know what their options are. I shared with them a recent report that argued that three of what will be the top ten jobs in 2020 have not even been invented yet, and that 12 percent of what will be the largest companies in the world in 2020 are not even around right now. When I graduated from college a decade ago, there was no Facebook. I remember meeting a gentleman at a conference back in 1998, a gathering of "young leaders." I was just finishing my time at junior college and was on my way to Johns Hopkins University to finish my undergraduate degree. We started talking and in his soft and singular way of speaking he told me that he and another friend of his were in the process of starting a company, a search engine. He tried explaining to me what that was, and I thought it sounded otherworldly. When I asked him the name of the company, my new friend Larry said he was calling it Google. It sounded ridiculous. I remember wishing Larry the best of luck but thinking, *I will never hear about that again.* Fifteen years and $400 billion later, Larry Page and Google have done quite well for themselves (and boy, did I miss out on the opportunity). In my defense, though, the future is hard to see. (But seriously, "Google"?) It's important to plan, but our plans should never become cages, especially plans we make at moments when we have imperfect information or when we're not even sure of who we are. Inflexibility can cause us to miss unexpected opportunities that suddenly appear, wave at us, and then fade when we fail to seize them.

Maybe we ask the question the wrong way. Maybe the question isn't "What do I want to do with my life?" but "Who do I want to be? What contribution do I want to make?" It's not even all about altruism. It's also about living the life that keeps you interested and engaged and passionate—and that leaves you feeling fulfilled.

When I speak at college campuses, one thing I try to do is work with the students to incorporate a service component into my visit, and really into their lives in an even more long-term way. We have asked students to find an issue in their community, their homes, and actually do something to address it. The goal is to make sure they understand and embrace that education is not about a degree to frame and throw up on a wall.

So I've worked with students from a variety of institutions, including UCLA, Northern Kentucky University, Kent State University, University of Minnesota, Georgia State University, Johns Hopkins University, Texas A&M, and Xavier University in New Orleans, among many others, and joined them in service projects in their respective communities. For the past two years I have spent days at the University of Louisville, a campus of striking beauty that, like countless other schools, is surrounded by neighborhoods marked by entrenched poverty. The service work that the students there engage in interacts with that larger community. In the balmy Kentucky fall, we conducted our Days of Service: everything from going door-to-door to encourage voter registration to inviting local residents to Network Nites that bring the university and community together. We visited the local Boys and Girls Club, and

I watched as the town-and-gown partnerships tied into a two-generation approach to empowerment. We spent the afternoon in the West End of Louisville, which is only miles away from the manicured and majestic grounds of the university, but whose working-class and middle-class residents were surrounded by empty lots and dilapidated housing. A common reaction of many colleges whose affluence abuts the poverty of their neighbors is to disengage, to simply warn students to "stay away," for fear that the school will develop a reputation for not being a safe place. But not at Louisville.

Led by an indefatigable faculty member named Christy Metzger, I witnessed Garrett Seay, a young man whose father passed away when he was young, like mine did, give a room-warming smile and a high five to each young man who answered a math question correctly. I spoke with Caitlin Gilmore, who shared laughs with students at a lunch table about her college experience, with each courageous and contagious anecdote dispelling the students' myths and fears. She told me that when she first entered the university she spent most of her time on campus, but now she was fully realizing that the blessing of her experience is about much more than just partying and the campus world. "Once I started to become more involved in the community and volunteer work *outside* of U of L, I immediately felt more complete. Participating in community service with my teammates, fellow colleagues, and the community members who we meet at the service projects is a blessing in itself."

I had the pleasure of meeting Lashawn Ford, who is the first one in her family to ever go to college, and now has a GPA of nearly 4.0. She did not grow up privileged in the traditional sense of the word, but her home was one of high expectations—the same expectations she enforces with the students she works with in Upward Bound, a federally funded program that helps students prepare for higher education. She knows what it is like to have others who don't know you make judgments about you. She knows what it is like to have some people meet your success with skepticism or even dismiss it altogether. "I became a mentor, tutor, and most importantly a friend to all of the students," she told me. "I don't want a student to feel that they can't go to college because of their grades, test scores, or criminal record. I want these students to come to college and prove everyone who ever doubted them wrong."

I was touched by Katie Faith's testimony about how during her first semester at the University of Louisville she volunteered at local schools in Jefferson County as part of a class called American Diversity. She was told to observe the students as if she were an anthropologist trying to gain an understanding of race and social dynamics. But it was going deeper that gave her a true understanding and purpose. Those class-sponsored visits turned into a full passion when she started to understand that "those kids" were actually "our kids," that our interconnectedness is real. She now wants to devote her life to kids and to supporting their hopes and dreams, even those whose current vision may look more like a confused kaleidoscope. She says: "I made sure they knew the importance of going to school, and telling the teachers if anything was wrong, but most important believing in themselves. Just believe in yourself, and know that somewhere, there is always going to be someone who is going to love you just as much as you love yourself."

■ ■ ■

A few years ago I learned about something called the "first year experience," or FYE, that is now available to first-year college students at many colleges all over the country. The program's directors select a book and have the entire freshman class read it before coming on campus; once there, the new students have discussions about it. I love this concept, because the truth is that a college's freshman class is made up of people with a wide assortment of backgrounds, interests, and philosophies. It is tough to establish common ground when you have such a diversity of students and perspectives. But with FYE programs, the students walk onto campus with a common intellectual project: to read a book and think critically about it.

During these experiences, I was struck by the fact that for many students in this country the true first-year experience is that they never actually complete their freshman year. Nationally, 34 percent of students who begin their freshman year will not complete that year or return for their sophomore year. Instead, many find themselves with minimal college credits (if any) and debt they now have to pay back. We are doing a better job of getting our young people out of high school than ever before, with more than 70 percent of U.S. students matriculating at a college or university after graduating from high school—the seventh-highest rate among the twenty-three developed countries that are members of the Organization for Economic Cooperation and Development (OECD). But only two-thirds of those end up graduating, the second-worst success rate among OECD nations. Overall in the United States, if you factor in community colleges, the percentage of students who graduate drops to 53 percent. To compound the problem, even many of those who finish lack the social capital and connections needed to compete in the job market once they leave school. Heartbreakingly, over 40 percent of those who graduated from college in 2013 were, at the time of this writing, either unemployed or underemployed.

If a student has difficulty making it past freshman year, generally it means that he or she will go no further in college. There is no simple reason for this, but there are three main sources of the trouble: financial (students are unable to handle the financial burden of higher ed, or something changes in their family that makes completing difficult), academic (students still need remedial work and are not yet academically prepared for higher education), and social (the most common reason, this is when the social transition to higher education and a new environment proves to be too challenging).

Having witnessed firsthand the struggles—and the potential—of first-year students and the importance of that first year in ensuring that students complete school, I decided to start BridgeEdU, a platform that looks to reinvent the freshman year. BridgeEdU partners with local universities and restructures how the freshman year is administered, allowing students a better on-ramp to success. Our scholars complete core academic classes and engage in real-world professional and service internships. They also work with coaches in small cohorts to smooth their transition into college and continue to work with them throughout their collegiate career, whether at the school they do their BridgeEdU year with or at any other school around the country that they transfer to, in order to ensure academic and career success.

I saw how in my own academic journey it was the holistic nature of learning that helped make the academic foundations actually mean something to me. Without the academic course work, I never would have received the credential of a college degree. Without my internship and externship experiences, I would have never made the necessary connections or been able to apply my academic course work to real-world settings. Without the service learning, I never would have understood why any of this stuff matters and what it means to be a global citizen. All of these things must be incorporated in order for someone to be considered truly educated. The ability to complete college opened doors I hadn't even imagined. It helped me to see the world in a way that I did not know was possible. I want to make sure that all students—those who are the first in their family to go to college, lower-income students, military veterans, and all others—share in not only that sense of completion but also that feeling of freedom. Higher education historically has been for only 20 percent of this country, but decades ago we started taking steps, from the GI Bill to an array of grants, scholarships, and loan programs, to ensure that college was more accessible to all students. Today, however, when we see the extraordinary number of students who make it into college but don't finish, it suggests that the challenge isn't just getting kids into college but keeping them there.

BridgeEdU's first group of students includes some who are the very first in their families to go to college, and some whose families have a long history of sending their young people to college. Some graduated from high school last year; some graduated three years ago and are giving college a second chance. Some went to public high schools, and others went to private schools. The only thing they all have in common is that they will complete their freshman year with academic classes and work experience under their belt at a fraction of the cost of a traditional public or private university. It's been stirring to watch the excitement of our students, their parents, their high school guidance counselors, employers, and community service leaders. Now I work daily to make sure we fulfill our mission with as many students and communities as possible.

Amid all this excitement, I haven't forgotten that there are still risks. It's true that after six years, only 40 percent of new start-ups are still around, and for social-minded enterprises the number is even lower. But I have learned from many people, including those profiled in this book, that you don't do things because they are easy. Nothing done with that motivation is worth doing. There are rare times in our lives when we find ourselves doing things because they need to be done—and something in us calls out to do it ourselves. That's a sign that we may have found the work of our lives. We will accomplish this mission. And not because someone gave me permission, but because I finally gave myself permission.

■ ■ ■ ■ ■ ■ ■ ■ ■ ■ ■ ■ ■ ■ ■ ■ ■ ■ ■

The Mentor

MICHAEL HANCOCK
Mayor of Denver, Colorado

The summer of 2012 was one of the hottest recorded in Denver's history. On Thursday, July 5, the mercury climbed to 99 degrees at Denver International Airport, making it the fourteenth day in a row that the Mile High City had seen temperature at or above 95 degrees.

The streak easily bested the old record of twelve consecutive days of 95+ degrees, set between July 2 and July 13, 1874. Those fourteen days in 2012 also represent the eighth-longest streak of days over 90 degrees since Denver began keeping records in 1872. The oppressive heat beat down on the city with a force that nobody was shaded from.

It was also one of the "hottest" summers for a completely

separate reason. While overall crime had been lowered, a hand-ful of incidents shook the city to its core.

A drive-by, random shots, two dead. Another man walking down the street shot dead by different shooters. The fatal shooting of a police officer at a public event when she thought she was breaking up a brawl between two men; it turned out to be the result of gang violence.

The summer of violence took a personal toll on the city's chief executive. Mayor Michael Hancock knew the police officer who was killed, but he also "knew" the young people responsi-ble for her death—because in many ways he had been one of them himself.

Michael Hancock, handsome and confident, with a disarm-ing smile, knows how thin the line is between where he is and where he came from. He and his twin sister, Michelle, are the youngest of a brood of ten, including three sets of twins. Michael didn't see much of his military father, who was stationed in Ger-many, until he was about seven and his father was rotated state-side. "He drank a lot and came home one day and said, 'I want a divorce.' The only memories I have of him between then and the next time I saw him, when I was about nine or ten, are of his voice on the phone. I remember watching my mother's frustration at getting just $175 for child support, and even that would be inter-mittent."

With his father gone, the family fell into the downward spiral of poverty that haunts single mothers. His mother, Scharlyne, deter-mined to give her kids a home, ran into the stone wall of discrimination, "not only as an African American but as a woman. All she wanted was to find a clean place for us. Every six months we were moving, and I didn't know it was because the lease was up. My sister and I were babies and were with her a lot. I remember this one landlord asking, 'Where's your husband?' She said, 'I'm divorced,' and he said, 'You gotta have a husband.' He wouldn't even talk anymore."

After two years of rootless survival, the family landed a duplex in a public housing development. But the years of instability took their toll. "Before I was in fourth grade I was in seven different elementary schools. There was no way to develop relationships. Today, we'd probably be the kids that would be identified as behind academically. My twin sister struggled mightily and was in special ed. I don't know why I was able to keep up academically. Even as I went through school, I remember there were challenges for me, and I got speech therapy and tutoring in reading and writing.

"My biggest fear growing up was that Mom would leave us. She could barely feed us and keep the lights on. Why would she stay? There were times she'd pull up to our duplex and I'd see her sitting in her Buick Century with her left hand on the door and her right hand to her cheek, unable to face us because she had no money for food. We'd all be hungry or facing living in a house with no lights or heat. Many days the only meal I got was at school. I'd gorge and get sleepy."

At least they were all together. His sister Karen—the fourth born but the first to graduate from high school—took care of Michael and his twin sister, making sure their clothes were clean.

Still, trouble trailed the Hancock clan. One brother was gay and died of AIDS when Hancock was twenty-six. One sister spent a lifetime battling drug and alcohol abuse. One brother did time for armed robbery, and this was after he went to college briefly after getting an athletic scholarship. "He was so into the social life and girls he couldn't function," Hancock recalls. "He was so intense about track and field and football, he became a superstar. He was also so intense about life that drugs were his only escape. One day someone called me and said, 'Turn on the news.' There was a picture of my brother after the crime. It was captured on video. It was drug abuse; he wasn't in his right mind."

Another brother assaulted a police officer with a deadly weapon when he was living in Texas with Hancock's father. His sister Karen, the one who raised Hancock and his twin sister and who Hancock says "was like a mother to me," was shot and killed by a boyfriend when she broke off the relationship.

"My mother is an amazingly resilient woman. She was always pretty sensitive and it hurt her to the core. But she never surrendered. She never stopped loving any of her kids regardless of what they did. She never gave up on herself or her kids," Hancock recalls. "I didn't realize it then, but I see now how cruel the world was to her. Without question, she was one of my primary inspirations."

After the tragic shootings in Denver that summer, he convened a group of fourteen gang members whom the police had already identified as some of the most challenged and at-risk in the community. They were well-groomed and good-looking, and some came to the meeting in suits and ties. But none of them was smiling. There was a great deal of pain and anger on their faces. For the first forty-five minutes, the most loquacious of them all, Kim— who had a baby face but "looked like you wouldn't want to meet her in a dark alley or a bright park"—answered every question. "Finally I interrupted her," says Hancock, "and I said, 'I have sat across this table from world leaders, some of the most successful business leaders, and none of them is as articulate and smart as you are. How did you end up in this place?'"

She started to cry, he remembers. "I said, 'Why are you crying?' She said no one had ever told her that. How are you supposed to believe when no one ever tells you you're worthy, you matter? In every instance they were crying out for help."

He "adopted" the kids. "God had a plan that day. He wanted me to intervene in the lives of these people. *Worthy*—that word just came out of my mouth. Every Saturday at 8:00 A.M. I had a prayer meeting over the phone with a group of men—we all get on the phone and someone leads us in scripture and someone else leads us in prayer. One day I told these guys this story and they said, 'There's your ministry and it's called Worthy.'"

Kim is pregnant, he tells me. "The pain she felt [earlier in her life] will prepare her appropriately and she'll be a more dedicated parent than most people who've never been through hard times. There are a lot of services to help someone like Kim. Part of the power of coming from where I've been is to know and acknowledge the potential in someone. She's a survivor."

He's determined to match up the kids with fourteen men and women who will mentor them—not, as Kim said, take them for ice cream once a month, but really be there. As Hancock says, "This is a direct reflection of my life. I'm here today because of the people who came into my life."

Among them is his wife of nineteen years, Mary Louise, who has known Michael since middle school. They started dating in high school. A professional singer who gigs with her band and performs in theatrical productions, Mary Louise is also a former youth diversion officer for the city. She has been much more than his loving wife and companion. She has also been the fuel and the architect behind his professional ascension. The couple were always passionate about service but were never sure about what exactly that meant. Michael spent much of his career prior to politics working in public service, but it was Mary Louise who gave him the motivation and permission to bring his gifts to the electoral stage.

Prior to running for office, he headed the city's Urban League, a huge responsibility for anybody but additionally daunting considering that he was only twenty-nine years old when he first took on the role. As the new director of programming, Hancock and his underpaid, overworked, but inspired team started building programs, and eventually he got promoted to vice president. "We narrowed our focus to help our clients become more self-sufficient. That was the plan. Job training, placement, home ownership. We said no to some programs, not because they weren't worthwhile, but because they weren't part of our mission. We focused on primary school education and primary school academic support."

Hancock built a multimillion-dollar institution, set up tutorial programming, and hired staff. His strategic plan was to build ten after-school programs in six years, "and it only took four. We built a whole youth department around summer camps in after-school programs. When I left in 2003, we served thirty thousand people a year on a $2 million budget."

Leaving the Urban League was not easy for him, but he felt that God was pulling him to another calling. He decided he wanted to run for office. "During my time at the Urban League, I realized the importance of good governance. A great deal can be done from the outside to impact communities. But having a reliable partner on the inside makes it that much easier." His wife supported the idea. She was behind his city council run because "it fit us well," says Michael. "It was a good opportunity. We loved what we got to do. It was flexible and let me take the kids to school every day. It fit our young family. Mayor? Not so much."

But after being a councilman for almost eight years and president of the Denver City Council for two terms, he knew where his next responsibilities lay. He decided he wanted to run for mayor of his hometown.

While he'd built a political résumé, he felt that his life had prepared him for this next set of challenges. He wanted to provide the same type of example and support to young people that he had so heavily relied on when he was growing up.

In the sixth grade, in the wealthy white school Hancock was bused to every day, he was a member of a little "gang." "We'd bully other kids in school, play tricks on them," he recounts. "There were white kids in our group, too, so that's why they didn't call us a gang. I got in trouble in sixth grade. For all the things I'd done, though, I hadn't ever been referred to the principal's office. I talked a lot and was class clown.

"One day I kept talking after the teacher threatened to send me to the principal. I threw a fit, tossed over desks, threw things on the floor. I made matters worse. I had tears and snot flying all over the place," Hancock says, laughing at the memory. The teacher took him to the principal's office. "When we got there, she told the principal, 'This young man is the best student in my class. He's just very emotional right now.' Miss Lott lifted me up. She said, 'I think he could be a speaker at the school's continuation ceremony.' She could have thrown me under the bus. But she didn't. She saved me and turned my life around."

Even then Hancock had demonstrated a drive for social justice and an uncanny knack for creating coalitions. "He's never been shy about expressing a desire to be part of something," says Stephanie O'Malley, his deputy chief of staff. "Part of Michael's attraction is that he's so personable. He has no hesitation whatsoever about going up to somebody and having a conversation, or just inquiring about someone's health and welfare—not wanting anything other than to be a partner in communications."

Young Hancock spearheaded a community tutoring center, recruiting kids from his high school to teach at it; he went on the speaking circuit, evangelizing for education and preaching an anti-drop-out message.

Hancock parlayed his accomplishments into a flourishing college career at Hastings College in Nebraska, but he had Denver on his mind. He'd just finished his freshman year when he wrote to Mayor Federico Peña explaining how much he wanted to be a summer intern, and why. He didn't expect a reply. "I was in my dorm room and someone said, 'There's someone on the phone for you.' It was Peña, on the pay phone in my hallway."

Years later, after completing a number of internships and achieving a graduate degree, Hancock began working at the National Civic League, helping to develop and implement strategic plans to deal with economic issues and to boost civic engagement for communities and nonprofits nationally.

By the time he was elected to the Denver City Council, Hancock had cemented his public service and education bona fides. Much of that was born of his faith, according to O'Malley, Will Alston, who is another old friend who works on special projects with him, and Hancock himself.

"Michael comes with a sense of godliness about him," says O'Malley. "Very in tune and in touch with his faith. I believe that his faith is a huge factor in how he manages his role as mayor. I always tease him and say, 'If this doesn't work out for you, there's always a role in the ministry.'"

Alston, who met Hancock back in his Urban League days, observes, "What role does faith play? I think it's one of the principal tenets of who he his. You don't get to turn that faith off. There are implications for people of an administrative policy that flows directly from that faith."

Late one Friday afternoon, a black SUV is hurtling down the highway, ferrying Michael Hancock, Denver's forty-fourth mayor, to his Green Valley Ranch home. He forgot his formal wear for the evening's two events, and time's of the essence, as he's supposed to be at the Botanic Gardens around six o'clock. However, he's going to be late for the Fête des Fleurs gala.

The big car slows, then swerves into the driveway of a tidy, deceptively large two-story house with a two-car garage. Hancock bolts inside the house; the driver and the security guard riding shotgun shake their heads and smile.

In just a few minutes Hancock emerges transformed, dapper in a formal black suit and crisp white shirt, showing no trace of a long, sweaty day of back-to-back meetings. Hancock is primed for the annual big-money fund-raiser in the Botanic Gardens' gorgeous Japanese gardens. There's a palpable surge of energy when he hikes himself into the car, carefully handing off the white dinner jacket he'll wear later to the Urban League's yearly cele-bration.

The SUV drops him off at the Botanic Gardens gate, where at-tentive aides grab him, speak in his ear about who is where and what's coming up, and guide him into the crowd in the newly ex-panded Japanese garden. Hancock has the gravitational pull of the sun, with well-wishers drawn by his genuine good nature and ear-nest interest. Suave-looking men going gray at the temples extend well-manicured hands to shake his, ask how this or that project is coming along, and give him a thumbs-up about the city's progress before Hancock moves on. Model-thin women in easily recogniz-able designer labels or vintage kimonos flash megawatt smiles and mention the stunning gardens. He cheerfully mentions to one that it would be really nice if there were more opportunities for less-advantaged kids to come and enjoy them. Then, with a smile, he disappears into the next cluster of donors.

The open-bar cocktail hour comes to an end, a gong sounds, and everyone drifts over to an enormous tent tricked out to bring the Japanese *hana matsuri* (festival of flowers) to Denver, complete with giant origami centerpieces. Now seated, the crowd bursts into applause when Hancock bounds onto the stage. He's charming, jokey, and earnest by turns. He congratulates the donors for turn-ing the Denver Botanic Gardens into a world-class, globally recog-nized educational and cultural institution. Again he mentions how great it would be if more kids, especially from underserved neigh-borhoods, could experience the wonders of the gardens. "It would be fantastic, wouldn't it?" he says, to applause. He's a cheerleader with a mission.

That done, he's down off the stage, wending his way through the crowd, patting shoulders, pausing to pose for a photo, as he heads toward the main building, where aides have stashed his change of outfit.

He leans over and whispers that events like this renew his faith not simply in the city and its progress but in his own decision to serve the city with all of his heart. It is a homegrown, organic faith that took root in his family, was nourished by his experience, and has fueled his drive.

On the way to his next event, he pulls up his calendar and adds a reminder to give Kim a call tomorrow to check on her.

7

■ ■ ■ ■ ■ ■ ■ ■ ■ ■ ■

The Lesson of the Family

Remember to Live

There's a phrase in Latin, *memento mori*, which translates to "remember you will die." It was used to describe symbolic representations of death that, for example, a seventeenth-century European might have in his home: a decorative skull on the mantel, or a painting of petals falling from a flower. Memento mori were meant to remind their owners not of death but of life: they were constant, silent reminders to make our time here on earth matter. We all collect memento mori without even realizing it, not necessarily as art, but in the form of experiences that remind us that life is fleeting and valuable. But as we go through our days, as our routines resume, we forget the lessons that seemed so life-changing at the time they occurred to us.

In the least morbid way possible, this book is intended as a kind of memento mori, a reminder that at every stage of our lives we must make our time here on earth matter.

■ ■ ■

I was guest-cohosting *Morning Joe* one morning, the MSNBC sta-ple that kicks off the cable channel's morning programming. Sit-ting with Willie Geist, a good friend and one of the most talented people in television, I looked over the schedule of events and saw that Harry Belafonte was going to be a guest in the eight o'clock hour. Harry Belafonte was revered in my home when I was grow-ing up. Of Jamaican descent, he introduced the world to his unique West Indian mix of fun-loving calypso and soulful ballads. He was also a heartthrob and a fine actor, and his combination of talents made him a star. But my grandparents' admiration for him went past his Jamaican heritage, his smooth baritone, or, in my grand-mother's case, his tight pants. They admired him because he was passionate about making his celebrity *mean* something.

What many didn't realize was that when Harry Belafonte was not entertaining crowds, he was supporting many of the important civil rights issues of the day. When Martin Luther King, Jr. needed someone to bail him out of the Birmingham jail, it was Harry Belafonte who came to his aid. Belafonte staked his personal wealth and risked his career to support Dr. King and the civil rights move-ment. Indeed, Belafonte suffered professionally: he was blacklisted and targeted by the FBI. But he never stopped. His activism con-tinued for decades, helping raise money for humanitarian inter-ventions all over Africa, working to bring down apartheid, and speaking out against American wars, including the war I'd fought in myself. He was a brilliant entertainer who leveraged his fame and wealth for the things he believed in, even when it cost him. He was a model of activism, humanitarianism, and fearless dissent.

As Mr. Belafonte slowly strode onto the set, his still-regal frame, smooth skin, and youthful features belied the fact that this was a man in his mid-eighties. He smiled, showing off the legendary grin that had won him millions of fans. We shook hands, and soon we were live on the air. He was talking about the new book he had completed about his life. He spoke about his entertainment career, but the conversation quickly turned to politics and the midterm elections that were fast approaching. He spoke with more passion about health disparities and economic inequality than he did about his performances at Radio City or Carnegie Hall.

When it came time for me to pose a question, I asked him where his undying passion for social issues had come from. Was it his immigrant history? Maybe his interracial marriage helped to shape his outlook? Was it living through the civil rights era and seeing how many of the people who were listening to his songs were still drinking from separate water fountains and eating at separate food counters?

He broke out into his famous grin again and softly chuckled. He told me it was just more fun to live that way.

That wasn't the answer I'd been expecting.

"Think about it," he continued. "Some celebrities wake up and call their accountants. I wake up and call Nelson Mandela. Who do you think has a more interesting life?"

I've traveled all over the country speaking to different groups—schools and civic organizations, nonprofits and businesses—about my first book, but inevitably the conversations would turn to the subject of success. People wanted to know what I thought the difference was between my life and the life of the other Wes Moore, why he was in jail for life and I was here in front of them now. I didn't have a clear answer. I thought a lot of the difference came from the people who'd helped me along the way; the other Wes didn't have the network of support I've had that has guided me along. The reasons for *that* are complicated. Part of it had to do with the cruel elimination of government programs of the sort that would've allowed the other Wes's mother to complete college. Part of it had to do with the other Wes's father choosing not to be a positive force in his life. Part of it had to do with the explosion of the drug trade in the inner city, a phenomenon that captured Wes and his older brother. Part of it had to do with the lack of support the other Wes had in school and at other critical junctures of his life when he needed help but instead found rejection, punishment, and isolation.

The more I talked about it, the more I realized that so much of success doesn't come from the individual and his or her boot-straps, but from the network of individuals that make up our communities, large and small.

Martin Luther King, Jr. was an extraordinary man, but he needed Harry Belafonte to bail him out and help support his family—and Harry stepped up to the call, which enabled King to do some of the extraordinary things we credit him for today. I owe everything in my own life to other people: the Rhodes Scholarship, which I owe to the efforts of my family and mentors; my time in Afghanistan, where my survival depended on my fellow soldiers and Afghan allies; the inspiration and guidance I got from those kids in Mississippi, from Ramón, from the people I met in Oxford and Washington. I owe all of it to other people who stepped up to serve in ways large and small—people who saw themselves as links in the chain of humanity, reaching out and connecting to the next link, binding us together.

■ ■ ■

I find a certain poetry and pride in the fact that after all of these years—wondering as I wander, as Langston Hughes would say—I have found some of my most satisfying work as a storyteller.

My father died when I was so young, but I knew his story as well as I knew my own. He was tall with a deep voice, and he dreamed of becoming a TV reporter. He hoped to follow in the footsteps of groundbreaking journalists such as CBS newsman Ed Bradley. Dad graduated from Bard College in 1971, and after holding a series of training jobs around the country, he returned to Maryland to host his own public affairs radio show. He met my mother when she applied and won a position as his writing assistant. Dad's signature sign-off for his show was, "This is Wes Moore. Thanks again, and we'll talk next time." I know how amazed and proud Dad would be to see me now: hosting programs on PBS and the Oprah Winfrey Network, talking to people on radio stations across the country.

My work expands as a father, as a husband, as a vet, as a journalist, and as a youth advocate. When my plate feels full to the point of spilling over, I try to remember that these are all roles I have chosen—not out of obligation or out of fear, but out of purpose, out of passion, and out of love. When people ask me now "What is next?" or "What will you do with the remainder of your life?" I don't feel a need to rush to an answer. I used to be intimidated by questions like these, and felt obligated to find an answer that would impress the people around me, even if I'd just met those people seconds earlier. That pressure has been released because I no longer feel the desire to force an answer simply to placate the interest of others. There is no "thing" I search for. I want to live a life that matters. I want to leave behind me a legacy of some kind. And, as Mr. Belafonte put it, I want to live an interesting life. That's the work I've chosen and wherever it hides itself, I've made it my task to search it out.

I also try to remind myself that while there is always a big-picture ambition or goal on the horizon, it's important to savor the little moments—the ones that will never come my way again. My father died in front of me when I was just months from my fourth birthday, so when I was five years old we went to live with my grandparents, and my grandfather Papa Jim became the primary man in my life. My grandfather had a deep respect for the rules, which is why it was so surprising that he broke his own rules and let me stay up way past my bedtime to watch game six of the 1986 World Series. My mother, a young widow at the time, was working three jobs, and my sisters had to go to sleep. But when my grandmother insisted that I too should go to bed, lest I be sleepy for school the next day, my grandfather—in a rare act of defiance—overrode her.

There was "his chair" in the living room, a white recliner that no one else could touch. I sat on the floor beside him. Papa Jim sat in the chair leaning back as the game headed toward what seemed like a disappointing close for the Mets. Mookie Wilson was up at the plate, taking confident practice swings, staring down the Red Sox pitcher on the mound, who was one out away from giving the Red Sox their first championship in more than eighty years. Mookie hit a very weak ground ball to first base that on any day would have been a routine out. But somehow the ball dribbled between the legs of Bill Buckner, the bushy-mustached Red Sox first baseman, and rolled into right field. His error led to a Mets run, and the Mets eventually won that game, and then went on to win the World Series. I still recall my grandfather's look of disbelief at that miraculous ending to game six: he was first shocked, then excited, then joyful. We hugged as if we were on the field together.

I say my grandfather was his own man, and baseball illustrates this as well as anything else. He grew up in Jamaica, where the game of choice is cricket. He was passionate about cricket as a boy, but from the moment he came back to the United States, the moment that he became officially and forever an American, baseball was his sport, and he showered on it all the love that he felt for the nation that had given birth to the game. We lived in the Bronx, just miles away from legendary Yankee Stadium, but my grandfather had no regard for the Bronx Bombers. His allegiance was to the Mets, and he didn't care what kind of ribbing he took from neighbors and friends. I don't know for sure what it was about the Mets; maybe it was because of an allegiance to a previous New York team, the Brooklyn Dodgers, who with Jackie Robinson were the first team to allow African Americans to play professionally. But I am inclined to think that my grandfather loved the Mets for being the scrappy working-class fan favorites, the perpetual underdogs to the golden-boys Bronx Bombers. For men like my grandfather, so brimming with possibility and yet so unseen by society at large, the Mets were a metaphor for hope.

When I was six years old, my grandfather told me that he had a surprise for me. Papa Jim's work as a minister in Brooklyn meant that there was little money for the kind of extras that boys my age dreamed of. So it was a thrill, and a bit of a shock, when my grandfather told me that he had gotten us tickets to a Mets game. It was my first live baseball game. Our boys were playing the San Diego Padres, and everything about the day was magical. Sitting next to him as he watched his beloved Mets that day, eating my first ball-park hot dog, observing as he filled out the box score with meticulous detail and efficiency—it was my own field of dreams. My grandfather had dedicated his life to the church, and I know that it is slightly sacrilegious to suggest that God might have rigged the game for his benefit. But I can't imagine what our day would have been like if the team had lost our first game at the stadium. Luckily, I'll never know: the Mets won, 4–3.

For as long as he lived, my grandfather and the way he lived his life inspired me to be better. To never be afraid of difference or of being "different." To cherish time with family and friends. He and my grandmother showed me that true heroism doesn't come with a job description or job title. It doesn't have to come with awards or citations. Airports might not be named after you; parks might not have a plaque with your signature emblazoned on it. Heroism is simply the idea of living your life with the passion that it deserves. It's knowing that independent thought and love-inspired vision are the greatest gifts we have been given, and that the chance to serve is the truest way of saying thank you. It's understanding that at some point everybody will die, but not everybody lives.

Appendix

■ ■ ■ ■ ■ ■ ■ ■ ■ ■ ■ ■ ■ ■ ■ ■

DOING THE WORK

As I said at the outset, this is not meant to be a prescriptive book. Instead I've tried to make a circumstantial, narrative case about how to build a life that matters, using my story and the stories of others. While the lessons in the stories are implicit and largely there for inspiration, going back over those stories with the questions on the following pages in mind might help you to start building your own plan for finding your work in life.

DANIEL LUBETZKY

Daniel Lubetzky's company KIND LLC is a New York City–based maker of snack bars that are carried nationwide by such retailers as Starbucks and Whole Foods. The company makes more than $30 million a year in revenue and has inspired more than twenty thousand acts of kindness. Here are some of the ways that Daniel's creation of what he calls a "not-only-for-profit" company might inspire your own work.

1. In his story Daniel says, "What I love is creating new stuff. The money is way secondary." If money wasn't a factor, what might you be inspired to create?
2. You can't talk to Daniel for ten minutes without him mentioning the word "fun." What's the most fun part of your job? When was the last time you had fun at work? Is there any way to inject some fun into the work you do now?
3. Adeena Cohen noted that at KIND, "we say 'and' instead of 'or': economically sustainable *and* socially impactful, healthy *and* tasty." Is there something about your work life that you've long considered an either/or situation? How can you add "and" to your life instead of "or"?
4. Daniel credits his parents' friendliness with giving him the personality he needed to be an entrepreneur. How could being more outgoing—introducing yourself to a stranger, inviting a coworker you don't know very well to lunch—help increase your chances of success?

5. Daniel says that he prefers to talk about impact rather than profit. If you were as successful as you could possibly imagine, what would you do to give back? How would you incorporate charitable giving into a "not-for-profit-only" business model?

JOE MANKO

1. Joe talks about his first year in Teach for America and how many of the first-year teachers had been so successful in other endeavors, but felt like failures in the classroom. Have you ever had an experience where, unexpectedly, you found yourself struggling in a professional environment? What are the lessons you can take from Joe and your experience?

2. In his story, Joe talks about the "end-of-the-year amnesia" he got during the summer break from teaching. Most jobs don't offer that kind of break, but if you could take a mental break from work, what could you push to the back of your mind that would help you better enjoy the work you do now?

3. When Joe was recruited to be a principal, he didn't feel ready for leadership. Is there something you're holding back from professionally because you don't feel ready?

4. Sonia Askew, one of the principals who mentors Joe tells him, "If you're not getting the answer you want, you have to stay with it until you do. These are kids you're fighting for." What in your life are you not getting right now? What is so worth it to you that you'll fight until you get the answer or outcome that you want?

DALE AND JOHN

Dale and John's story involves the post-traumatic stress disorder that can result from having served in a war. But the dynamics of their friendship, and how they both experienced and tended to their wounds, have elements in common with the experiences of many more people. These are some of the questions that their story raised for me.

1. Dale and John's friendship has been a guiding force in their lives for over a decade, both on and off the battlefield. Do you have a friend who just gets what you're going through and what you're feeling, no explanations necessary?

2. How can you lean on this friend to help you find the work that fills you up? How has this friend inspired and aided you in the past?

3. Dale lost both legs to the IED, but both he and John agree that John has suffered more and healed more slowly because his wounds couldn't be seen. Do you have wounds that aren't visible to the eye? What have you done, and what might you do, to tend to those wounds that are visible only to you?

ESTHER BENJAMIN

1. Esther Benjamin gets up at four every day and hits the ground
    running at five. If you're not already an early riser, what could
    you do with an extra hour in the day? Is there some dream you
    could pursue if you slept a little less and got up earlier?
2. One of the words that Esther uses to describe herself is "fear-
    less." In what parts of your life are you fearless? In what areas
    would you like to be more courageous?
3. Esther talks about how her family was able to come to the
    United States when violence was disrupting the lives of so
    many back in Sri Lanka. She says guilt, anger, and regret are
    emotions she's not interested in because they aren't useful or
    productive. Can you think about the things in your own life
    that have caused or could cause you guilt, anger, or regret?
    Does reading Esther's story give you a sense of how to not
    hang on to those emotions, to see them as unproductive and
    to some extent let them go?

CARA ALEY

1. The Aley story is in some ways a story about large ambitions that didn't quite pan out—but it is not a story of defeat. What do you think setbacks—even failures—can teach us? What have failures in your own past taught you, and how can you use those lessons in your next project?

2. One of the possible reasons for American Mojo downfall was that they tried to do too much too soon with the company. Are there ways to simplify your own work to make sure that you haven't taken on more than you can handle, but without undermining the core values of the project?

3. American Mojo was a social enterprise—a for-profit business with higher goals than simple profit. Is there a way to add a social dimension to whatever work you're doing, even if your primary goal is to make money? Is there a way to add a sustainable financial element to your work, even if your primary goal is philanthropic?

MICHAEL HANCOCK

1. Michael Hancock was a self-described bully and member of a "little gang" that got him in trouble as a school-aged child. But a teacher saw his potential despite the trouble he caused, and "turned my life around." Can you remember a time in your life when someone made a similar intervention on your behalf? Have you ever had the opportunity to do the same for someone else?

2. People around Hancock point to his being "personable" as the key to his success—his willingness to seek out advice and listen. Are there people in your life right now who might be a good "partner in communication" for you, to help you with whatever project you're working on in your life? What holds you back from approaching them?

3. Through all of the ups and downs and challenges of Hancock's life, his faith has been a constant. One colleague said of his faith: "You don't get to turn that faith off. . . . Administrative policy flows directly from that faith." We all don't have religious faith as part of our lives, but we all have deeper values at the core of our lives. How do your deepest values flow into your work?

Acknowledgments

■ ■ ■ ■ ■ ■ ■ ■ ■ ■ ■ ■ ■ ■ ■ ■

To those who are reading this, I first want to thank you. For taking the time to pick up the book, to read it, internalize it, and hopefully do something with it. I truly believe that the point of this process, or any other narrative process is not simply to write a book. It's to spark a bigger conversation. Something lasting. And I thank you for allowing me to share my journey with you, and for your sharing your journey with me. It means more than you know. To my God, who woke me up every morning, tucked me in every night, and made every day worth living, thank you. You have blessed me more than I deserve and more than I need. To my family, who every day motivate me and inspire me. You do not simply allow me to be myself, you allow me to be a better me. A more enlightened me. A more grateful me. Time passes, but my love for you doesn't. To my ancestors who have long ago left us for their homegoing, Mama Win, who remains the matriarch of my family and my soul, my mom whom I strive every day to be more like because you are my benchmark for humanity, and my aunts, uncles, cousins, step-cousins, friends, and all of those who I share no blood relation with but are as much "family" as anyone else, thank you. Nothing I do could be done without you. Nothing I believe in would make sense if it were not for you. To my siblings: Nikki, Shani, Jamaar, Earl, and Rita, thank you for not just your support, but unwavering love. It, and you, mean more to me than you know. And to Shani specifically for being part sister, part editor, I am blessed to have so much talent in my family tree. To my kids: Mia who is my heart and James who is my soul. Your smiles block out everything. You make both my best days and worst days better, and in you I have all the meaning I could ever ask for. To Dawn, you are my everything. There is no better, or more appropriate way to put it.

To Linda Loewenthal, once again it is my honor to have you at my side. You are an amazing agent, but more important, a cherished friend. To Cindy Spiegel and Julie Grau, its not easy to find people who take their talents and use it for good. The world is a better place because of your "work," and I am a better person because you are in my life. To Chris Jackson, *everything* in this book, from the framework to the meaning to the title, has the marking of C. J. on it. In many ways, I try to be the man you think I am, and I try to be the man you already are. And to the entire Spiegel and Grau team (family), Barbara Fillon, Karen Fink, Sally Marvin, Tom Perry, Leigh Marchant, Erika Seyfried, and Annie Chagnot, thank you for pushing me, driving me, inspiring me. Veronica Chambers and Anne Adams, your fingerprints are all over this manuscript. The fact that you shared yourself and your talents with me mean more than you know. Thanks for making the time to make my work better.

There are so many friends and inspirations I have to thank for this. I feel bad trying to even begin naming them in fear of leaving many off, but to Mustafa Riffat, Tom and Stephanie Pellathy, Donald and Godly Davis, Justin and Angela Brandon, Sean and Tish Fox, Tim Lancsek, Ty Hill, Colonel Michael Murnane, Colonel Michael Fenzel, John and Marcy McCall-MacBain, Ken and Tricia Eisner, Howie and Susie Mandel, David and Debbie Roberts, Derick and Kendra Ausby, Dan and Avery Rosenthal, Dr Frank Reid, Tom and Andi Bernstein, Darrell and Felice Friedman, Tommy and Christy Ransom, Jarvis and Stacey Stewart, Ericka Pittman, Keith and Dia Simms, Marlon and Toni Fletcher, Tonya Carr, Mark and Lois Vann, Rachel Monroe, Jeshahnton Essex, William and Sharon Rhoden, Fagan Harris, Ryan and Sarah Hemminger, Jan and Larry Rivitz, Luke and Marina Cooper, Sheldon Caplin, Dr Freeman Hrabowski, Kurt Schmoke, Dr Jay Perman, Alec and Felicity Ross, Jeff and Nikki Harris, Julian and Michelle Harris, Ian Klaus, Seth and Chelsea Bodnar, Bob and Dawn Wylie, Melissa Chang, Kristen Mitsinikos, Lou and Rosemary Oberndorf, David and Laura Kleinhandler, Wally Boston, Tim Weglicki, Gary and Steven Erlbaum, Shanaysha Sauls, Robert and Benis Reffkin, Adrian Talbot, Ann Edelberg, Willie and Christina Geist, Greg and Katherine Tucker, Roger Kamau, Zach and Andrea McDaniels, Hassan Murphy, Larian Finney, Tom Wilcox, Harrison Hickman, Molly Fowler, Nick Kouwenhoven, Tisha Edwards, Tiphane Waddell, Billie Malcolm, Bill and Leah Ferguson, Joe Jones, David Warnock, Colm OComartun, Ulysses Archie, David Buckson, Kristin Chaney, Codi Chavis, Tajae Griffin, Tyson Sanford-Griffin, Brandon Sears, Tristan Tanner, James Watkins, Chanel Whisonant, Chandler Younger, and Joe Picharillo, thank you and God bless you all.

I have the most amazing group of friends, family, mentors, and guides. I am thankful for you all. And to those I did not mention in this section, please know how much you still mean to me. I stand here because you have always stood with me.

I will love you all now and always. . . .

Elevate,

Wes

Resource Guide

■ ■ ■ ■ ■ ■ ■ ■ ■ ■ ■ ■ ■ ■ ■ ■ ■

THE WORKERS

While not an exhaustive list, these organizations, companies, NGOs, religious organizations, advocacy groups, and social enterprises epitomize the "work" being done every single day—you might find among them someone whose work connects with your own. Get in touch to support, volunteer, or collaborate.

NAME	LOCATION	ABOUT
"I Have a Dream" Foundation	New York	The "I Have A Dream" Foundation is working to ensure that all children have the opportunity to pursue higher education. They empower children in low-income communities to achieve higher education by providing them with guaranteed tuition support and equipping them with the skills, knowledge, and habits they need to gain entry to higher education and succeed in college and beyond.

100Kin10	National	100Kin10 is a networked approach to providing America's classrooms with 100,000 excellent STEM teachers by 2021 while supporting tens of thousands more. Through unique, ambitious commitments, their 150+ partners are together fueling the creation of the next generation of innovators and problem solvers.
4-H	National	4-H is the nation's largest youth development and empowerment organization. More than 6 million 4-H youth in urban neighborhoods, suburban schoolyards and rural farming communities stand out among their peers: building revolutionary opportunities and implementing community-wide change at an early age.
AchieveMinneapolis	Minnesota	As the nonprofit partner of the Minneapolis Public Schools (MPS), AchieveMpls serves as a bridge between MPS and the broader community—businesses, foundations, nonprofits, government agencies and individuals—providing information and opportunities to engage as volunteers, employers, funders, advocates and advisers.
Advanced Home Energy	California	Advanced Home Energy partners with homeowners who are interested in going green and offers a wide range of home energy efficiency solutions.
Advocates for Children and Youth	Maryland	Advocates for Children and Youth improve the lives and experiences of Maryland's children through policy change and program improvement.
Alter Eco	California	Alter Eco works with dozens of small-scale agricultural cooperatives in the Global South to provide a fairer deal and market access for small farmers. Alter Eco offers a large range of exquisite Fair Trade, Organic and Carbon Neutral foods.

America SCORES	National	A national nonprofit, America SCORES serves 8,000 students at more than 150 public and charter schools in 14 major cities. Their mission is to inspire urban youth to lead healthy lives, be engaged students, and have the confidence and character to make a difference in the world. They achieve this mission through daily after school and summer programming, which combines soccer, poetry and service-learning.
America's Promise Alliance	National	America's Promise Alliance is devoted to helping to create the conditions for success for all young people, including the millions currently being left behind. Their work is powered by the belief that all children are capable of learning and thriving, and that every individual, institution and sector shares the responsibility to help young people succeed.
American Dental Education Association	National	The mission of ADEA is to lead individuals and institutions of the dental education community to address contemporary issues influencing education, research and the delivery of oral health care for the health of the public.
AmeriCorps	National	AmeriCorps engages more than 75,000 Americans in intensive service each year at nonprofits, schools, public agencies, and community and faith-based groups across the country. Since the program's founding in 1994, more than 900,000 AmeriCorps members have contributed more than 1.2 billion hours in service across America while tackling pressing problems and mobilizing millions of volunteers for the organizations they serve.
Andean Naturals	California	Andean Naturals acts as a bridge between South American quinoa farmers and US food companies. It facilitates the growth of the organic and fair-trade quinoa market while improving the lives of over 4,500 small family farmers through increased income, technical assistance and sustained demand.

Animal Experience International	Ontario, Canada	AEI has a mission to help animals around the globe by matching clients with animal-related volunteer opportunities at sanctuaries, wildlife hospitals, animal clinics and conservation projects.
Apolis Holdings LLC	California	Apolis, which translates as "global citizen," is a living and breathing social enterprise that equips and empowers people through opportunity.
Association for the Study of Higher Education	Nevada	ASHE promotes collaboration among its members and others engaged in the study of higher education through research, conferences, and publications, including its highly regarded journal, The Review of Higher Education.
Association of Independent Maryland & DC Schools	Maryland	AIMS supports its member schools by providing professional development, accreditation services and public advocacy.
Astellas US LLC	Illinois	Astellas seeks to improve the health of people around the world through the provision of innovative and reliable pharmaceutical products.
Atayne	Maine	Atayne makes high-performing outdoor and athletic apparel from 100% recycled materials.
Aunt Bertha, Inc.	Texas	Aunt Bertha, Inc. provides a simple way to find and apply for need-based food, health, housing and education programs
Autism Speaks	National	Autism Speaks is the world's leading autism science and advocacy organization, dedicated to funding global biomedical research into the causes, prevention, treatments and a possible cure for autism. They strive to raise public awareness about autism and its effects on individuals, families, and society, and work to bring hope to all who deal with the hardships of this disorder.
Baltimore Corps	Maryland	A frontier of social change, Baltimore is shaped and strengthened by citizens, communities and change makers. Baltimore Corps grows the impact of leading social change organizations while building a movement of inspired leaders.

Banister's Leadership Award	National	Banister's Leadership Academy provides stability, engagement, education and advocacy to help Omaha youth and families, schools, and businesses build resiliency and human capital.
Banking on Our Future	National	BOOF is Operation HOPE, Inc.'s, premier financial education program for youth in underserved communities. It provides on-the-ground and online financial literacy programs that teach children basic money skills.
Bark House	North Carolina	Highland Craftsmen Inc. designs, manufactures and sells all-natural Bark House brand architectural elements to building, design and furniture professionals as well as individuals.
Bay Area Medical Academy	California	Bay Area Medical Academy offers job-oriented training in high-growth, high-demand, specialized areas of the healthcare field and prepares individuals for successful long-term careers.
Beartooth Capital	Montana	Beartooth Capital is a leading impact investment fund manager whose mission is to generate strong investment returns, real conservation results, and community benefits.
Beneficial State Bank	California	Beneficial State Bank builds prosperity in its community through beneficial banking services delivered in an economically and environmentally sustainable manner.
Best Buddies	International	Founded in 1989 by Anthony K. Shriver, Best Buddies is a vibrant, international organization that has grown from one original chapter to almost 1,700 middle school, high school, and college chapters worldwide.
Big Brothers Big Sisters	National	Big Brothers Big Sisters provides children facing adversity with strong and enduring, professionally supported one-to-one mentoring relationships that change their lives for the better, forever. This mission has been the cornerstone of the organization's 100-year history.

Blue Engine	New York	Blue Engine prepares students in low-income communities in New York City to succeed in postsecondary education through exposure to rigorous and personalized high school coursework. The organization recruits bright recent college graduates to work as teaching assistants in public high schools serving low-income communities.
Blue Garnet	California	Blue Garnet is a strategy and management consulting firm that works with organizations to create lasting social change by harnessing the combined power of business acumen and social impact.
BluPlanet Recycling, Inc.	Alberta, Canada	BluPlanet Recycling, Inc. is a Calgary based multi-family residential and commercial recycling collection service provider.
Boys & Girls Clubs of America	National	Boys & Girls Clubs of America has enabled young people most in need to achieve great futures as productive, caring, responsible citizens. Today, more than 4,100 Boys & Girls Clubs provide a safe place, caring adult mentors, fun, friendship, and high-impact youth development programs on a daily basis during critical non-school hours.
BridgeEdU	Maryland	BridgeEdU is an innovative college completion platform that addresses the college completion and career placement crisis by reinventing the Freshman Year in a way that engages students in real-world internships and service learning opportunities.
Brotherhood/ Sister Sol	New York	Brotherhood/Sister Sol is a Harlem-based organization with a mission to empower black and Latino young women and men to think critically and become leaders in their communities. It offers a range of enriching educational after-school opportunities and summer programs designed to help youths realize and achieve their individual potential as well as increase their ability to empower others within their community.

Buy the Change	Michigan	Buy The Change works with NGO's and small craft co-operatives throughout the developing world to source fairly-traded, woman-made accessories, jewelry and home décor products, many of which are made from ecofriendly, up-cycled materials.
Byoearth	Guatemala City, Guatemala	Byoearth's goal is to have all degradable waste be transformed into benefit for people, the environment, and earth through vermiculture and vermicomposting.
CAP Global	California	CAP Global develops and commercializes novel pharmaceuticals for global populations through local partnerships.
Cass Community Social Services	Michigan	The Detroit-based agency works across the city in areas of concentrated poverty providing programs for food, health, housing and jobs.
CDI Lan	Sao Paulo, Brazil	CDI Lan generates income & employability through education & training in low-income communities by providing access to high social impact solutions through internet cafes.
Center for Urban Families— Responsible Fatherhood	Maryland	The Baltimore Responsible Fatherhood Project assists low-income Baltimore fathers in becoming actively and positively engaged in their children's lives.
ChangeIt	Ontario, Canada	ChangeIt is a giving program that enables users to support their favorite causes with every electronic purchase.
Channel Islands Outfitters	California	Channel Islands Outfitters is a Santa Barbara and Channel Islands based paddle sports outfitter and fitness center.
Charity: Water	International	Charity: Water is a non-profit organization bringing clean and safe drinking water to people in developing nations.
Chicago Youth Centers	Illinois	CYC invests in youth in underserved communities in Chicago to help them discover and realize their full potential.

Citizen Schools	National	Citizen Schools partners with middle schools to expand the school day for children in low-income communities, mobilizing a team of educators and volunteers to help children discover and achieve their dreams.
City Year	National	City Year is an education-focused, nonprofit organization that partners with public schools to provide full-time targeted intervention for students most at risk of dropping out. In 25 communities across the United States and through two international affiliates, our teams of young AmeriCorps leaders support students by focusing on attendance, behavior, and course performance through in-class tutoring, mentoring, and after school programs that keep kids in school and on track to graduate.
Cleveland Metropolitan School District	Ohio	The Cleveland Metropolitan School District envisions 21st Century Schools of Choice where students will be challenged with a rigorous curriculum that considers the individual learning styles, program preferences and academic capabilities of each student, while utilizing the highest quality professional educators, administrators and support staff available.
Climate Smart	British Columbia, Canada	Climate Smart is a social enterprise that trains businesses and provides them with software tools to track and reduce their greenhouse gas emissions.
College Board	National	Each year, the College Board helps more than seven million students prepare for a successful transition to college through programs and services in college readiness and college success—including the SAT and the Advanced Placement Program.
College for Every Student	New York	CFES is a nonprofit organization committed to raising the academic aspirations and performance of underserved youth so that they can prepare for, gain access to, and succeed in college.

College Now Greater Cleveland	Ohio	College Now provides Greater Cleveland students with guidance and access to funds to prepare for and graduate from college.
Comet Skateboards	New York	Comet Skateboards is the leading manufacturer of high performance, eco-friendly skateboards.
Communities in Schools	National	Communities in Schools is a nationwide network of passionate professionals working in public schools. For more than 30 years, the organization has been helping students achieve in school, graduate and go on to bright futures. Their mission is to surround students with a community of support, empowering them to stay in school and achieve in life.
Community Action Partnership of the Greater Dayton Area	Ohio	Community Action Partnership of the Greater Dayton Area is committed to eliminating poverty and promoting self-sufficiency by providing various programs and services for individuals and families
Community Wealth Partners	Washington D.C.	Community Wealth Partners offers strategy and implementation services to nonprofit organizations and philanthropic foundations, partnering with them to design and implement innovative approaches to growth and sustainability.
Congressional Black Caucus Foundation	National	The CBCF takes a proactive stance in determining policy initiatives that facilitate the economic and social well-being and wellness of black men in the United States.
Connecticut Association of Nonprofits, Inc.	Connecticut	The mission of CT Nonprofits is to support and strengthen nonprofit organizations in building and sustaining healthy communities in Connecticut.
Cooperative Home Care Associates	New York	CHCA is the nation's largest worker-owned cooperative, providing high-quality home care services to elders and individuals living with disabilities—primarily African-American and Hispanic residents of the South Bronx, Harlem, and Washington Heights.

Council Fire	Maryland	Council Fire is a world-class management consulting firm working with clients to "operationalize" sustainability and harness the power of information to drive competitive advantage and success in both the public and private sectors.
Council for Advancement and Support of Education	National	CASE helps its members build stronger relationships with their alumni and donors, raise funds for campus projects, produce recruitment materials, market their institutions to prospective students, diversify the profession, and foster public support of education.
Council of Great City Schools	National	It is the special mission of America's urban public schools to educate the nation's most diverse student body to the highest academic standards and prepare them to contribute to our democracy and the global community.
d.light	California, China, Kenya	d.light manufactures and distributes solar lighting and power products providing access to reliable, affordable, renewable energy for nearly 30 million people in 60 countries.
Delight Hearing Aid	Seoul, South Korea	Delight manufactures and distributes hearing aids at affordable prices.
Divine Chocolate Limited	Washington, DC	Divine Chocolate Limited is a leading purveyor of Fair-trade chocolate.
Dolphin Blue	Texas	Dolphin Blue is an online retailer of ecologically sustainable products for use in commercial and home offices.
Down to Earth Farmers Markets	New York	Down to Earth Markets curates and manages approximately 20 farmers markets in Westchester County, Rockland County, and four of the five boroughs of New York City.

DREAM (Directing Through Recreation, Education, Adventure, and Mentoring)	Vermont, Massachusetts	DREAM combines best practices from both mentoring and community development programs to create a unique experience for college students and children. During weekly meetings at the colleges, the students work as a team to provide mentoring activities to children in both individual and group settings. Volunteer mentors also work with parents from the developments to ensure that their local DREAM program is inclusive, safe, and inspiring. The long-term relationships that develop between the children and mentors are the foundation of the programs and provide a means for children to engage in positive risk-taking, see new perspectives, and take advantage of community resources.
EarthKeeper Alliance	California	EarthKeeper Alliance is dedicated to the conservation, preservation, restoration and thoughtful development of large tracts of land previously slated for large-scale development.
Eastern Carolina Organics	North Carolina	This farm-owned business markets and distributes wholesale Carolina organic farm produce to retailers, restaurants and buying clubs.
Echale	Mexico City, Mexico	Echale is a social housing production company that delivers affordable homes to communities through the implementation of innovations in construction technology and finance, streamlining the self-build process and strengthening social inclusion.
Ecotrust Forest Management	Oregon	Ecotrust Forest Management is a forest-land investment management and advisory services company that generates long term value for both investors and society by facilitating positive environmental outcomes and supporting job creation in rural communities.
Education Funding Partners	Colorado	Education Funding Partners provides Fortune 500 corporate marketing sponsorships exclusively for major public school districts.

El Paso Independent School District	Texas	EPISD is dedicated to the success of its students and supports them in all ways to ensure that they will excel upon gradua-tion.
Emerge	Tennessee	Emerge Financial Wellness is workplace-based financial wellness program that partners with employers to help their workers plan their financial futures.
Enterprise Charter School	New York	The Mission of the Enterprise Charter School is to provide students with the knowledge, skills, and dispositions to grow and problem-solve, giving them the re-sources to lead and succeed in the school and the community at large.
Enviro-Stewards	Ontario, Canada	Enviro-Stewards Inc.'s engineers & scien-tists serve as sustainability catalysts for in-dustrial, commercial and institutional facilities. As such, they stimulate increased margin on sales while reducing environ-mental footprints and improving social conditions.
Expeditionary Learning	New York	Expeditionary Learning (EL) is a leading K-12 education non-profit that is raising the bar on student achievement through its rigorous project-intensive curriculum and practical, inspiring professional devel-opment that engages students and ener-gizes teachers. EL students demonstrate critical thinking, academic courage and re-silience, and possess the passion and abil-ity to contribute to a better world.
Exploring the Arts	New York	ETA was initially created to support the NYC public high school, Frank Sinatra School of the Arts, which opened in 2001. After the success of the Sinatra School and seeing the impact firsthand of a qual-ity arts education, ETA expanded to work with existing public high schools.

Eye to Eye	New York	Eye to Eye pairs college students with learning disabilities with middle school students with similar learning disabilities as a way to show young kids that they are not alone in their disability and can be successful. Through weekly after school projects, mentors teach mentees how to advocate for themselves to get the tools they need in the classroom. The disabilities that Eye to Eye address are mainly dyslexia, ADHD and other language-based disabilities.
Facing History and Ourselves	International	Facing History and Ourselves provides ideas, methods, and tools that support the practical needs, and the spirits, of educators worldwide who share the goal of creating a better, more informed, and more thoughtful society.
Fans Without Footprints	New York	Fans Without Footprints leverages the power of sports and the passion of its fans to benefit the environment by offering the opportunity to join with their favorite team to support local green projects in the community.
Farmland LP	California	Farmland LP acquires conventional farmland and converts it to organic, sustainable farmland.
Federation of Families for Children's Mental Health	Maryland	FFCMH focuses on the issues of children and youth with emotional, behavioral, or mental health needs and their families.
Feelgoodz LLC	North Carolina	FeelGoodz LLC is a global eco-conscious footwear brand driven by core values of social responsibility and transparency
Feronia Forests LLC	Massachusetts	Feronia acquires and sustainably manages natural hardwood forest properties in the U.S.
Fidelity Charitable	National	Fidelity Charitable is an independent public charity, established in 1991 with the mission to further the American tradition of philanthropy by providing programs that make charitable giving simple and effective.

FINAE	Mexico City, Mexico	FINAE is a social impact financial institution created to give more students access to private university education.
For Inspiration and Recognition of Science and Technology	National	FIRST has designed accessible, innovative mentor-based programs to build self-confidence, knowledge, and life skills while motivating young people to pursue opportunities in science, technology, and engineering.
FlipGive	Ontario, Canada	FlipGive provides a digital platform that connects brands to the $200+ billion fundraising market, converting customers into a sales force to raise money.
FutureProof	Louisiana	FutureProof is a nationally recognized interdisciplinary firm that provides full-service sustainability master planning, green infrastructure design and development, integrated water management landscapes, LEED and technical consulting.
Gateway to College National Network	National	Gateway to College National Network offers a second chance for high school dropouts (ages 16-21) and students on the verge of dropping out to earn a high school diploma while also earning college credits.
GE Foundation	National	The GE Foundation empowers people by helping them develop the skills they need to succeed in a global economy.
GEAR UP	National	GEAR UP provides six-year grants to states and partnerships to provide services at high-poverty middle and high schools. GEAR UP grantees serve an entire cohort of students beginning no later than the seventh grade and follow the cohort through high school. GEAR UP funds are also used to provide college scholarships to low-income students.
Girls Who Code	New York	Girls Who Code programs work to inspire, educate, and equip girls with the computing skills to pursue 21st century opportunities. They aim to provide computer science education and exposure to 1 million young women by 2020.

Give Some-thing Back	California	Give Something Back Office Supplies is California's largest independent office sup-ply company, with giving back to commu-nities integral to its core mission and purpose.
Giving U Inspirational Lives Through our Youth	North Carolina	Giving U Inspirational Lives Through our Youth is a youth development organiza-tion that works together with the commu-nity to better the lives, build the confidence, and create a positive future for youths labeled at-risk and delinquent.
Global Kids, Inc.	New York	Founded in 1989, Global Kids, Inc. works to develop youth leaders for the global stage through dynamic global education and leadership development programs. GK in-spires underserved youth to achieve aca-demic excellence, self-actualization, and global competency, and empowers them to take action on critical issues facing their communities and our world.
Good.Must.Grow. LLC	Tennessee	Good.Must.Grow. LLC provides strategic marketing for socially responsible busi-nesses and nonprofit causes.
Graham Windham	National	Graham Windham strives to make a life-altering difference with children, youth and families affected by abuse, neglect and delinquency by providing each child with a strong foundation for life: a safe, loving, permanent family and the opportu-nity and preparation to thrive in school and in the world.
Green Living Enterprises	Ontario, Canada	Green Living Enterprises is a full-service media, marketing, custom content pro-vider and events company that has in-creased public awareness of environmental issues and inspired per-sonal action through print publications.
Green Retire-ment Plans	California	Green Retirement Plans helps businesses, nonprofits and their employees harness the power of their retirement plan assets for good.

Greenway Medical Technologies, Inc.	South	Greenway Medical Technologies, Inc. delivers the innovative information solutions providers need to better manage quality, efficient care and achieve improved population health.
Greyston Bakery	New York	The company aims to hire the hard-to-employ and is known for its "open hiring" practices, where anyone can sign up regardless of background.
GRID	Virginia	GRID is a free magazine providing upbeat news and resources to the greater Richmond area.
Grounds For Change	Washington	Grounds for Change is a certified organic coffee roaster specializing in 100% fair trade coffee. They roast organic fair trade coffee that is grown in shaded conditions and offer comprehensive wholesale and fundraising programs.
Heart of Illinois United Way	Illinois	The Heart of Illinois United Way brings together people from business, labor, government, health and human services to address the community's needs.
Helping Hand Home for Children	Texas	Helping Hand Home provides residential treatment services, therapeutic foster care, adoption services, and an on-site charter school for children who have suffered severe abuse and neglect.
Higher Learning Commission of the North Central Association	Illinois	The Higher Learning Commission accredits degree-granting, post-secondary educational institutions in the North Central region.
Holton Career & Resource Center	North Carolina	The Holton Career & Resource Center offers programs that provide both training and instruction focused on traditional and emerging industries.
Home Care Associates	Pennsylvania	HCA has dedicated itself to a quality care through quality jobs mission. By providing quality home care jobs, HCA works to ensure quality care across the Philadelphia metropolitan area for elders and people with disabilities.

Homewood Children's Village	Pennsylvania	The mission of the Homewood Children's Village is to simultaneously improve the lives of Homewood's children and to re-weave the fabric of the community in which they live.
Horizons National	National	Begun in 1964, Horizons National Summer Programs are a network of high-quality academic enrichment programs that pro-vide long-term deep engagement to low-income public school students. The hands-on approach is designed to fuel a life-long passion for learning, using a blend of high-quality academics with arts, sports, cultural enrichment, and confidence-building challenges, particu-larly swimming.
Hybrytec Solar	Antioquia, Colombia	Hybrytec Solar designs and installs solar energy systems for health centers, fishing villages, schools, hotels, and private cus-tomers.
IMentor	New York	IMentor is a school-based mentoring pro-gram that empowers high school students in low-income communities to graduate high school, succeed in college, and achieve their ambitions.
Impact First	Tel Aviv, Israel	Impact First invests in early stage health-care, edtech, agritech, and cleantech so-cial enterprises.
Impact Makers	Virginia	Impact Makers is a management and tech-nology consulting company based in Rich-mond, Virginia that contributes 100% of their net profits to charities.
Imprint Capital	California	Imprint Capital is an impact investment firm that creates and manages high per-forming impact investment portfolios for foundations, families, and financial institu-tions.
Independent Educational Consultants Association	National	IECA is the professional organization for independent educational consultants working in private practice

Indigenous Designs	California	Indigenous Designs is a leader in organic and fair trade clothing. Their clothing supports thousands of artisans in the most remote and impoverished regions of the world.
Ingage Partners	Ohio	Ingage Partners delivers information technology and management consulting services to help their clients successfully navigate business and technology change.
Institute for Responsible Citizenship	National	The Institute for Responsible Citizenship prepares high-achieving African-American men for successful careers in business, law, government, public service, education, journalism, the sciences, medicine, ministry, and the arts.
Jobs for America's Graduates	National	JAG is a state-based national non-profit organization dedicated to preventing dropouts among young people who are most at-risk. In more than three decades of operation, JAG has delivered consistent, compelling results—helping nearly three-quarters of a million young people stay in school through graduation, pursue post-secondary education and secure quality entry-level jobs leading to career advancement opportunities.
Juhudi Kilimo	Nairobi, Kenya	Juhudi Kilimo finances targeted agricultural assets for smallholder farmers and rural enterprises across Kenya. Operating exclusively in very rural areas, they give smallholder farmers access to the tools they need to scale up and succeed.
Junior Achievement	National	Founded in 1919, JA is the world's largest and longest running nonprofit economic education organization for students in grades K through 12. They currently reach 4.5 million students in 116 communities across the United States, empowering them to own their economic success through the promotion of financial literacy, work readiness and entrepreneurship.

Junior Chamber International	International	JCI encourages young people to become responsible citizens and to participate in efforts toward social and economic development, and international co-operation, good-will and understanding.
Kentucky School Board Association	Kentucky	KSBA enhances school board leadership by maximizing student achievement through superior support and services.
Kentucky Science and Technology Corporation	Kentucky	KSTC is an entrepreneurial company dedicated to enhancing the capacity of people, companies and organizations to develop and apply science and technology and compete responsibly in the global marketplace.
La Crosse Area Family YMCA	Wisconsin	At the Y, children and teens learn values and positive behaviors, and can explore their unique talents and interests, helping them realize their potential.
Latin American Youth Center	Washington, DC	LAYC is a nationally recognized organization serving all low-income youths and families across the District of Columbia and in Maryland's Prince George's and Montgomery counties. LAYC provides multilingual, culturally sensitive programs in five areas: educational enhancement, workforce investment, social services, art and media, and advocacy.
League of Minnesota Cities	Minnesota	The League of Minnesota Cities promotes excellence in local government through effective advocacy, expert analysis, and trusted guidance for all Minnesota cities.
Lifetouch Inc.	National	As the world's largest employee-owned photography company, Lifetouch is committed to building strong relationships, loyalty that lasts a lifetime, and memories that last forever.
Little Pickle Press	California	Little Pickle Press is a publisher of high quality, high impact media for children, dedicated to helping parents and educators cultivate conscious, responsible little people by stimulating explorations of the meaningful topics of their generation.

Lotus Foods	California	Lotus Foods works to help rice farmers earn a living wage while bringing healthier rice choices to consumers.
Majora Carter Group	New York	The Majora Carter Group offers pioneering solutions to concentrated environmental problems through economic development by way of public speaking engagements, workshops, and consulting services.
Mal Warwick Associates	California	Mal Warwick Associates help nonprofits and political organizations build long-term, mutually rewarding relationships with individual donors through integrated fundraising and marketing programs.
Management Leadership for Tomorrow	National	MLT is a national nonprofit that has made groundbreaking progress developing the next generation of African-American, Hispanic, and Native American leaders in major corporations, nonprofit organizations, and entrepreneurial ventures.
Manchester Bidwell Corporation	Pennsylvania	Manchester Bidwell Corporation's diverse programming combines to create empowering educational environments for adults-in-transition as well as urban and at-risk youth, enriching Southwestern Pennsylvania and, eventually, the world.
Manzimvula Ventures	British Columbia, Canada	Manzimvula Ventures is a values-based consulting firm whose purpose is to support organizations who choose to build socially responsible and profitable enterprises that profoundly impact their organizational communities and the individuals they affect in a compassionate and sustainable manner.
Massachusetts General Hospital	Massachusetts	Guided by the needs of patients and their families, Massachusetts General Hospital aims to deliver the very best health care in a safe, compassionate environment; to advance that care through innovative research and education; and to improve the health and well-being of the community.

Mayor's Workplace Mentoring Program	Maryland	MWPMP matches eighth through twelfth-grade youths from Baltimore's middle and high schools with Baltimore city employees/mentors.
McCormick & Company, Inc.	National	Building on a cultural foundation of concern for one another, McCormick is committed to making a positive difference in the global communities where we live and work.
Memphis Grizzlies Charitable Foundation	Tennessee	The Memphis Grizzlies Charitable Foundation is committed to serving Memphis youth through education and mentoring.
Mental Health Association of Connecticut	Connecticut	The Mental Health Association of Connecticut is dedicated to offering the latest mental health research, education and training to the community.
Metropolitan Group	Oregon	Metropolitan Group is a national strategic and creative services firm increasing impact for socially responsible businesses.
Mikado	Istanbul, Turkey	Mikado is a social enterprise committed to serving sustainable development and yielding social impact. They craft innovative models and solutions by creating partnerships among the private sector, civil society, academic institutions and international organizations.
Missouri Association for Community Action	Missouri	MACA is a statewide association of community action agencies fighting poverty in Missouri.
Moving Forward Education	California	Moving Forward Education provides tutoring and mentoring services for underserved students in the Bay Area.
Murex Investments	Pennsylvania	Invests venture capital in high-impact, early-stage learning tech and financial tech for the poor.

My Brother's Keeper	National	President Obama launched the My Brother's Keeper initiative to address persistent opportunity gaps faced by boys and young men of color and ensure that all young people can reach their full potential. Through this initiative, the Administration is joining with cities and towns, businesses, and foundations that are taking important steps to connect young people to mentoring, support networks, and the skills they need to find a good job or go to college and work their way into the middle class.
Namasté Solar	Colorado	Namasté Solar is an employee-owned cooperative that designs, installs, and maintains solar electric systems for homes, businesses, non-profits, and government entities.
NASPA	National	As a leading association for student affairs professionals, NASPA offers professional development training, events, and resources.
National Academy Foundation	National	The National Academy Foundation is a leader in the movement to prepare young people for college and career success. NAF has refined a proven educational model, which includes industry-focused curricula, work-based learning experiences, and business partner expertise from five themes: Finance, Hospitality & Tourism, Information Technology, Engineering, and Health Sciences.
National Association of Electrical Distributors	National	Electrical distributors buy thousands of products from hundreds of electrical manufacturers and then warehouse, sell, and deliver these products to their customers, making a better life for communities everywhere
National Council for Community & Education Partnerships	National	NCCEP works to increase access to higher education for economically disadvantaged students.

National Education Association	National	NEA is the largest professional organization and largest labor union in the United States, representing public school teachers, faculty and staffers at colleges and universities, retired educators, and college students preparing to become teachers.
National PTA	National	National PTA prides itself on being a powerful voice for all children, a relevant resource for families and communities, and a strong advocate for public education.
National School Boards Association	National	Working with and through our State Associations, NSBA Advocates for equity and excellence in public education through school board leadership.
National Urban Technology Center, Inc.	National	The Urban Tech aims to provide access to technology and training to address the widening computer literacy and achievement gap in inner-city communities. Its primary focus is to transfer educational tools to schools and community-based organizations nationwide for promoting life skills, academic performance, and workforce preparation among young people ages ten through nineteen.
Nebraska Association of Homes and Services for Children	Nebraska	NAHSC works to promote and improve quality in the continuum of care for Nebraska children and their families through advocacy, education, cooperative efforts among members, and effective communication between providers and the State of Nebraska.
Ned Schaub Consulting Social Change Strategy	California	NSC SCS facilitates and supports sustainability planning, philanthropic strategy, retreats and workshops, particularly for organizations in the healthcare and social service sectors.
Network for Teaching Entrepreneurship	National	NFTE provides entrepreneurship education programs to young people from low-income communities.
New Avenue	California	New Avenue is an online platform that sells architecture services, loans and construction to homeowners who want to add a second unit to their single family home.

New Neigh-borhoods, Inc.	Connecticut	NNI is a nonprofit housing developer and manager, dedicated to building, redeveloping and preserving low and moderate income rental and ownership housing
New Resource Bank	California	New Resource Bank supports businesses, nonprofits, and people that are pursuing innovative solutions to environmental, economic, and social challenges.
New York Cares	New York	New York Cares was founded by a group of friends who wanted to take action against serious social issues that faced the city in the late 1980s. It is the city's largest volunteer management organization, running volunteer programs for 1,300 nonprofits, city agencies, and public schools.
New York City Department of Education	New York	The New York City Department of Education is the largest school district in the US, serving 1.1 million students in over 1,800 schools.
Noel Levitz	National	A recognized leader in higher education consulting, Noel-Levitz is committed to helping institutions meet their goals for enrollment and student success.
Norman Chamber of Commerce	Oklahoma	The Norman Chamber of Commerce can provide information on city statistics, major employers, education, arts and culture, health care, community resources, recreation and entertainment, housing, and other relocation information.
North Carolina Partnership for Children	North Carolina	NCPC works to advance a high quality, comprehensive, accountable system of care and education for every child beginning with a healthy birth.
Northwest Evaluation Association	Oregon	NWEA is a non-profit organization working alongside member school districts to create a culture that values and uses data to improve instruction and student learning.
Npower Indiana	Indiana	NPower mobilizes the tech community and provides individuals, nonprofits and schools access and opportunity to build tech skills and achieve their potential.

NYC Outward Bound Schools	New York	NYC Outward Bound Schools transforms New York City's public schools and changes students' lives. They operate a network of public schools that engage students through a codified curriculum of real-world, hands-on learning that is relevant in students' lives and communities; their schools place an equal emphasis on character and academic development; and they also offer their signature Outward Bound programming to public schools that are not part of their school network.
Ohio Scholl Boards Association	Ohio	OSBA leads the way to educational excellence by serving Ohio's public school board members and the diverse districts they represent through superior service, unwavering advocacy and creative solutions.
Omaha Empowerment Network	Omaha	Their mission is to transform the City of Omaha into a great city, thriving and prosperous, where all citizens are engaged and empowered and have full access to the incredible opportunities. The Empowerment Network is a collaboration of residents, elected officials, neighborhood groups, community organizations, philanthropists, educational institutions, faith communities, governmental agencies, and businesses, working together to transform Omaha.
On Point	Tennessee	On Point exists to "build healthy teens," accomplishing this by giving teens in-depth knowledge, personal support, and the life skills they need to achieve a life of excellence.
One Earth Designs	Hong Kong, China	One Earth Designs develops and markets technology solutions, including solar ovens and generators, for those who lack access to clean and affordable energy.
One Pacific-Coast Bank	California	One PacificCoast Bank is an innovative, triple-bottom line, community development financial institution.

Operation HOPE	International	Operation HOPE is America's first non-profit social investment bank and a national provider of financial literacy and economic empowerment programs free of charge. At the core of HOPE's mission to eradicate poverty and empower the wealthless is a movement to establish "silver rights," or the right to financial literacy, access to capital, and equality of opportunity for all.
Pacific Northwest Kale Chips	Oregon	Pacific Northwest Kale Chips is a small-batch chip maker founded on the principles of delivering locally sourced, organic, and sustainable food to all sectors of society.
Palmetto	London, United Kingdom	Palmetto offers a fully integrated service to lead organizations toward cost-effective and sustainable solutions. Through customized planning and efforts to deliver tangible investment opportunities, they have delivered over $10 billion toward a clean energy future.
Participant Media	International	Participant is a global entertainment company founded in 2004 to focus on feature film, television, publishing and digital content that inspires social change.
Parties That Cook	California	Culinary events company that stages hands-on cooking events for corporate teams and private parties.
PBS	National	PBS and our member stations are America's largest classroom, the nation's largest stage for the arts and a trusted window to the world. In addition, PBS's educational media helps prepare children for success in school and opens up the world to them in an age-appropriate way.
Peckham, Inc.	Michigan	Peckham, Inc., a nonprofit community vocational rehabilitation organization, is a unique business and human services agency that values quality, diversity and performance.

Penguin Random House Speakers Bureau	National	The Speakers Bureau represents an unrivaled roster of speakers whose work is shaping national conversations—on and off the page.
Pennsylvania Housing Finance Agency	Pennsylvania	The Pennsylvania Housing Finance Agency works to provide affordable homeownership and rental apartment options for senior adults, low- and moderate-income families, and people with special housing needs.
PhilanTech	Washington D.C.	PhilanTech provides the PhilanTrack online grants management system—an innovative online grant proposal, reporting and management system that enhances accountability, transparency, and efficiency.
Piedmont Biofuels	North Carolina	Piedmont Biofuels is a community scale biodiesel operation that collects used cooking oil from area food service establishments and converts it into a clean burning renewable fuel.
Pioneer Investments	International	Pioneer Investments and its associates are actively involved in initiatives that support the education, build the knowledge and, promote the good health of children living around the world.
Project Repeat	Massachusetts	Project Repeat upcycles t-shirts into more fun and fashionable clothing accessories while creating jobs.
Project SEARCH	National	The Project SEARCH High School Transition Program is a unique, business led, one year school-to-work program that takes place entirely at the workplace. Total workplace immersion facilitates a seamless combination of classroom instruction, career exploration, and hands-on training through worksite rotations.
Prudential Financial Services	National	Prudential is committed to helping the underserved in our communities by eliminating barriers to financial and social mobility.

Publicolor	National	Through a multi-day, multi-year continuum of design-based programs that teach at-risk students how to think critically about their future and prepare for college and career, Publicolor is able to steer high-risk students from struggling to successful. Their philosophy is anchored in high expectations and the belief that, when students experience daily successes, they build the self-confidence necessary to achieve more in all areas of their life.
PwrdBy	California	PwrdBy develops community awareness and support for charity through photo-sharing apps on iPhone & Android.
Questol	Guatemala City, Guatemala	Quetsol provides affordable solar power to off-grid communities.
Re:Vision	Pennsylvania	Re:Vision Architecture is an architecture, planning, and consulting firm specializing in sustainable design and development.
Reach Out and Read	National	Reach Out and Read builds on the unique relationship between parents and medical providers to develop critical early reading skills in children, beginning at 6 months of age.
Reading is Fundamental	National	Reading is Fundamental motivates young children to read by working with them, their parents, and community members to make reading a fun and beneficial part of everyday life. RIF's highest priority is reaching underserved children from birth to age 8.
Renewal Funds	Vancouver, Canada	Renewal Funds is a social venture fund dedicated to delivering financial returns by investing in leading environmental and social mission businesses in Canada and the USA.
Rhode Island After School Plus Alliance	Rhode Island	RIASPA works with its partners to offer professional development to afterschool programs, improving their quality and advancing the field

Roadtrip Nation	National	Roadtrip Nation is a public television series and grassroots movement that encourages young people to hit the road in search of interviews with leaders who have defined their own distinct routes through life.
Rocking the Boat	New York	Rocking the Boat empowers young people challenged by severe economic, educational, and social conditions to develop the self-confidence to set ambitious goals and gain the skills necessary to achieve them. Students work together to build wooden boats, learn to row and sail, and restore local urban waterways, revitalizing their community while creating better lives for themselves.
Ron Clark School in Atlanta	Georgia	The Ron Clark School aims to empower youth to take charge of their own destinies.
Roshan	Kabul, Afghanistan	Roshan is Afghanistan's leading telecommunications provider.
RSF Social Finance	California	RSF offers investing, lending, and giving services that generate positive social and environmental impact while fostering community and collaboration among participants.
Scholarships, Inc.	National	Scholarships, Inc. provides students with the necessary financial resources to pursue higher education.
Schoolnet, Inc.	National	Schoolnet, Inc. is the leading provider of instructional improvement education software that increases student achievement, teacher quality and operational efficiency.
Sechler CPA PC	Arizona	Sechler CPA PC is a completely virtual accounting firm serving the tax and consulting needs of approximately 350 local, national and international nonprofit organizations.
Secondary School Admissions Test Board	New Jersey	SSATB provides unparalleled leadership and service in meeting the admission assessment and enrollment needs of schools, students, and families.

SEEDS	Pennsylvania	SEEDS is a green printing company composed of environmentally conscious, creative professionals with years of experience in the fields of printing, design, marketing, writing and editing, and world-class customer service.
SEQUIL Systems, Inc.	Florida	SEQUIL Systems, Inc. is a professional services firm that provides highly technical building commissioning, LEED program management, energy modeling and sustainability consulting services to the architecture, engineering and construction industry.
Sesame Workshop	New York	Sesame Workshop is the nonprofit organization behind Sesame Street, and their mission is to use the educational power of media to help children everywhere reach their highest potential.
SJF Ventures	North Carolina	SJF Ventures helps companies succeed by providing growth capital & assisting entrepreneurs with their challenges.
SLOWCOLOR	California	SLOWCOLOR is an integrated bottom line high impact clothing enterprise committed to revitalizing the use of age-old traditions to dramatically reduce the social, environmental and health impacts of textile manufacturing.
Social Enterprise Associates	New Mexico	Social Enterprise Associates is a consulting firm offering business acumen, managerial experience, financing opportunities, and practical research to business and community efforts seeking social good.
Social Good Network	Idaho	Social Good Network works at the confluence of cause and commerce, using its innovative software to create and measure the success of digital cause marketing campaigns for brands.
Social Venture Network	California	Social Venture Network is a nonprofit membership organization composed of socially responsible business leaders who are committed to creating a more just and sustainable world.

South Carolina Association of School Administrators	South Carolina	The mission of SCASA is to advocate for a worldwide education for the children of South Carolina and to provide leadership development for its members.
South Mountain Company	Massachusetts	South Mountain Company is an employee-owned design, build, and renewable energy company on Martha's Vineyard. The company plans and develops residential and commercial buildings, as well as designing and installing solar & wind energy systems and energy efficiency improvements.
Southern Association of Colleges and Schools	National	The mission of the Southern Association of Colleges and Schools is the improvement of education in the South through accreditation.
SpeakInc	California	An employee owned and operated company, SpeakInc has grown to become the largest speakers bureau in the western United States.
Special Olympics	National	Special Olympics is an international organization that changes lives through the power of sport by encouraging and empowering people with intellectual disabilities, promoting acceptance for all, and fostering communities of understanding and respect worldwide.
Step It Up, Inc.	Oregon	Step It Up, Inc. is an organization that connects career-oriented high school students with professional career internships during the summer and pays them a stipend/scholarship.
Stop Soldier Suicide	National	Stop Soldier Suicide is the first national civilian not-for-profit organization dedicated to preventing active duty and Veteran suicide.
Sunrise Community Banks	Minnesota	Sunrise Community Banks is in the business of developing strong communities that provide homes and jobs to their residents.

Sustainability Advantage	Ontario, Canada	Sustainability Advantage provides educational talks and resources to help lead a transformation toward a sustainable global society.
Taco Bell Foundation for Teens	National	Since 1992, the Taco Bell Foundation for Teens has enabled and inspired teens to graduate high school and reach their full potential through its programs, partnerships and direct financial assistance. They have provided educational and job training support to more than 1 million teens in communities across the country, awarding more than $42 million in grants and scholarships to more than 1,000 teen-serving organizations in the U.S.
Taharka Brothers Ice Cream Co.	Maryland	Taharka Brothers Ice Cream Co. is a for-profit and for-community social enterprise managed and operated primarily by college aged young adults.
TAS	Ontario, Canada	TAS is a real estate development company with a commitment to shaping beautiful cities.
Team Rubicon	National	Team Rubicon unites the skills and experiences of military veterans with first responders to rapidly deploy emergency response teams.
Texas Society of Association Executives	Texas	TSAE provides high quality educational, leadership, and professional development opportunities to association executives and supplier members, which enhances the performance of the organizations they represent.
The 6th Branch	Maryland	The 6th Branch is a nonprofit organization utilizing the leadership and organizational skills of military veterans to execute aggressive community service initiatives at the local level.

The ACE Mentor Program of America	National	The program's mission is to enlighten and increase the awareness of high school students to career opportunities in architecture, construction, engineering, and related areas of the design and construction industry through mentoring; and to provide scholarship opportunities for students in an inclusive manner reflective of the diverse school population.
The Arnold Development Group	Missouri	The Arnold Development Group is a purpose-driven real estate investment and development firm that creates sustainable mixed-use projects.
The Arthur M. Blank Family Foundation	Georgia	The Arthur M. Blank Family Foundation promotes innovative solutions to improve the lives of youth and their families, seeking results that move communities beyond what seems possible today.
The Big Blue Bike	Texas	Style-focused, quality clothing produced with disadvantaged communities and the environment in mind
The Bridge-port Child Advocacy Coalition	Connecticut	The Bridgeport Child Advocacy Coalition is a coalition of organizations, parents, and other concerned individuals committed to improving the well-being of Bridgeport's children through research, education, advocacy, and mobilization.
The Colorado Health Foundation	Colorado	The Colorado Health Foundation engages through grant-making, public policy, investing in evaluation, private sector engagement and communications outreach to make Colorado the healthiest state it can be.
The Eagle Academy Foundation	New York	The Eagle Academy Foundation is committed to the development of a network of all-male college-preparatory public schools (grades six through twelve) that educate and develop young men into future leaders committed to excellence in character, scholastic achievement, and community service. The foundation is focused on creating Eagle Academies in high-poverty communities with excessively high rates of incarceration.

The Foundation for International Community Assistance	International	FINCA is the innovator of the village banking methodology in microcredit and is widely regarded as one of the pioneers of modern day microfinance.
The Fund for Education Abroad	Washington, DC	The Fund for Education Abroad is committed to increasing the opportunities for dedicated American students to participate in high-quality, rigorous education.
The Keys Children's Foundation, Inc.	Florida	The Keys Children's Foundation provides financial support to non-profit organizations dedicated to providing programs that offer education, healthcare and recreation to disadvantaged children and their families living in the Florida Upper Keys.
The Morehouse Male Initiative	Georgia	Morehouse College plays an active role in conducting and disseminating research and best practices regarding the affirmative development of African-American males.
The New York Foundling	New York	The New York Foundling is one of New York City's oldest and largest children's charities and produces tangible results in the lives of thousands of vulnerable children and troubled youth every year.
The Paradigm Project	Colorado	The Paradigm Project is a low-profit limited liability company operating in cooperation with The Paradigm Foundation, whose collective mission is to create sustainable economic, social and environmental value within developing world communities.
The Raise Up Project	National	The Raise Up Project features an online hip hop and spoken word competition that awards educational scholarships to talented 15-22 year olds in an effort to reduce high school dropout rates.
The Steppingstone Foundation	Massachusetts	Founded in 1990, The Steppingstone Foundation develops and implements programs that prepare underserved students for educational opportunities that lead to college success.

The Stewpot Alliance	Texas	The Stewpot offers a safe haven for homeless and at-risk individuals of Dallas, providing resources for basic survival needs as well as opportunities to start a new life.
The Sustainable Law Group, PC	California	The Sustainable Law Group, PC serves as corporate counsel to nonprofits, businesses and estates.
TOMS Shoes	National	TOMS matches every pair of shoes purchased with a pair of new shoes for a child in need.
Town Hall South	Pennsylvania	Town Hall South is dedicated to bringing nationally and internationally acclaimed lecturers to the South Hills of Pittsburgh.
Training Magazine	Minnesota	Training Magazine is a 50-year-old professional development magazine that advocates training and workforce development as a business tool.
Trilium Asset Management, LLC	Massachusetts	Trillium Asset Management, LLC is the oldest independent investment advisor devoted exclusively to sustainable and responsible investing.
U.S. Dream Academy	Maryland	The U.S. Dream Academy focuses on three pillars: skill building, character building, and dream building. The overall goal is to nurture the whole child while changing attitudes about education.
United Way	National	United Way advances the common good by focusing on education, income and health—the building blocks for a good quality life. The United Way movement mobilizes millions to action and creates lasting changes in communities around the world.
United Way of Mass Bay	Massachusetts	To make the greatest impact possible, United Way aligns a network of more than 200 independent health and human service agencies under the same set of community goals.
United Way of Rhode Island	Rhode Island	United Way of Rhode Island works to help change thousands of lives across our state through education, income and housing.

United Way Worldwide	International	United Way Worldwide improves lives by mobilizing the caring power of communities around the world to advance the common good in the fields of education, income and health.
Vail Unified School District	Colorado	Vail Unified School District supports the parent of its students, so those parents can then provide a healthy environment for successful kids.
Veris Wealth Partners, LLC	New York	Veris Wealth Partners, LLC is a wealth management firm committed to helping align wealth with a customer's mission.
VH1 Save the Music	National	The VH1 Save The Music Foundation is a nonprofit organization dedicated to restoring instrumental music education programs in America's public schools, and raising awareness about the importance of music as part of each child's complete education.
VIF International Education	North Carolina	VIF International Education is the nation's largest J-1 teacher exchange sponsor and a provider of language immersion and global literacy programs.
VISIONS	New York	VISIONS is an 88-year old nonprofit vision rehabilitation and social service agency serving people of all ages with blindness and severe vision loss and their families. VISIONS consumers are primarily low income, from communities of color, with multiple barriers to success, speaking many languages. VISIONS serves over 6,000 individuals each year utilizing hundreds of volunteers and community partners, and all services are free of charge.
Voices for Children St. Louis, MO	Missouri	Voices for Children advocates for abused and neglected children and youth in St. Louis by representing their best interests in court and in the community.
Voices for Utah Children	Utah	Voices for Utah Children works to make Utah a place where all children thrive through health, school readiness, safety, diversity and economic stability.

W.S. Badger Co.	New Hampshire	W.S. Badger Co. manufactures Badger Balm and other USDA organic body care products.
Warby Parker	National	Warby Parker tallies up the number of eyeglasses sold and makes a monthly donation to nonprofit partners, who cover the cost of sourcing that number of glasses.
Water Power Group	Ontario, Canada	Water Power Group is a private power producer working in partnership with local and Aboriginal communities to develop small run-of-river hydroelectric projects in markets across North America, primarily in Ontario, Canada.
Wells Fargo Advisors	National	Through volunteer efforts and philanthropy of Wells Fargo Advisors as a whole and individual team members who are ready, willing, and able to participate, they are committed to building strong and vibrant communities, improving the quality of life, and making a positive difference in communities throughout the U.S.
Whiz Kids	Oklahoma	Whiz Kids is a faith-based, one-on-one volunteer tutoring and mentoring program that focuses on first through sixth-grade students who live in areas that have some of the highest drop-out rates and lowest socioeconomic levels in Oklahoma City.
Wisconsin Association of School Boards	Wisconsin	The Wisconsin Association of School Boards is a member-driven organization that supports, promotes and advances the interests of public education in Wisconsin.
Worldof-Money	New York	WoM is a New York City–based organization focused on improving the financial literacy of underserved youths ages twelve through eighteen. To this end, WoM has created a training institute consisting of workshops and activities designed to help students become financially responsible adults.
Wounded Warrior Project	National	Wounded Warrior Project works to foster the most successful, well-adjusted generation of wounded service members in our nation's history.

X-Runner	Lima, Peru	X-runner provides waterless toilets and waste management services to families that do not have standard toilets.
Yellow Leaf Hammocks	California	Yellow Leaf Hammocks are 100 % hand-woven, customizable hammocks that offer customers supreme comfort, strength and durability, along with a commitment to cultivating a sustainable economic opportunity for marginalized ethnic groups like the endangered Mlabri Tribe.
Young Presidents Organization	International	YPO connects successful young chief executives in a global network unlike any other.
ZocDoc	National	ZocDoc is an online medical care scheduling service, providing free of charge medical care search facility for end users by integrating information about medical practices and doctors' individual schedules in a central location.